Woe Is I

A GROSSET / PUTNAM BOOK

PUBLISHED BY G. P. PUTNAM'S SONS

NEW YORK

Woe Is I

The Grammarphobe's Guide to Better English in Plain English

Patricia T. O'Conner

For Stewart

A Grosset/Putnam Book
Published by G. P. Putnam's Sons
Publishers Since 1838
200 Madison Avenue
New York, NY 10016

Library of Congress Cataloging-in-Publication Data

O'Conner, Patricia T.
Woe is I : the grammarphobe's guide to better English in plain English /
by Patricia T. O'Conner.
p.   cm.
Includes bibliographical references and index.
ISBN 0-399-14196-0
1. English language—Grammar—Handbooks, manuals, etc.
2. English language—Usage—Handbooks, manuals, etc.   I. Title.
PE1112.028   1996   96-11473 CIP
428.2—dc20

Printed in the United States of America
9   10   8

Book design by Brian Mulligan

This book is printed on acid-free paper. ∞

Contents

Acknowledgments

Countless friends and colleagues helped make this book by contributing ideas, pointing out omissions, and sneering at my mistakes. I'm glad that I was able to provide you all with a socially acceptable outlet for your more aggressive impulses. Your patience and good humor were second only to mine, and I can't thank you enough.

I'm particularly grateful to those who read the manuscript: Laurie Asséo; David Feldman; Margalit Fox; Elizabeth Frenchman; Anita Gates; Neal, Margo, and Garth Johnston; Dimi Karras; Peter Keepnews; David Kelly; Eden Ross Lipson; Deborah Nye; Allan M. Siegal; Rachel Elkind Tourre; Gloria Gardiner Urban; Elizabeth Weis; and my unbeatable mother, Beverly J. Newman.

For their support, encouragement, and advice, I thank Michael Anderson; Michael Barson; Alida Becker; Brenda

Berkman; Tom Ferrell; Ken Gordon; Pamela and Larry Kellerman; Harvey Kleinman; Charles McGrath; Merrill Perlman; Michael Sniffen; Katlyn Stranger; Yves Tourre; Marilynn K. Yee; Arline Youngman; my sister, Kathy Richard; my encyclopedic father-in-law, Allen G. Kellerman; my agent, Dan Green; and Kate Murphy and Anna Jardine at Putnam.

Sam Freedman was generous with his time and advice, and passed along much valuable insight (especially about danglers) from his experiences as a reporter, an author, and a teacher. William Safire was kind enough to acquaint me with the invaluable Jeff McQuain, who expertly scoured the manuscript for errors. (Any boo-boos that remain are mine alone.) And this book couldn't have been written without the help of Jane Isay, my editor and publisher at Grosset/Putnam, whose idea it was in the first place.

Finally, my most heartfelt thanks go to my husband, Stewart Kellerman, for his conjugal as well as conjugational expertise. He put his own book aside many, many times to help me with mine. He's my best friend, and the best editor I know.

Introduction

We all come from the factory wired for language. By the time we know what it is, we've got it. Toddlers don't think about language; they just talk. Grammar is a later addition, an ever-evolving set of rules for using words in ways that we can all agree on. But the laws of grammar come and go. English today isn't what it was a hundred years ago, and it's not what it will be a hundred years from now. We make up rules when we need them, and discard them when we don't. Then when *do* we need them? When our wires get crossed and we fail to understand one another.

If language were flawless, this wouldn't happen, of course. But the perfect language hasn't been invented. No, I take that back—it has been done. There are so-called rational languages (like the "universal" tongue, Esperanto, and the computer-generated Eliza) that are made up, designed to be logical, reasonable, easy to speak and spell, to make sense. And guess what? They're flat as a pancake. What's missing is the quirkiness, as well as the ambiguity, the bumpy irregularities that make natural languages so exasperating and shifty—and so wonderful. That's wonderful in the literal sense: full of wonders and surprises, poetry and unexpected charm. If English weren't so stretchy and unpredictable, we wouldn't have Lewis Carroll, Dr. Seuss, or the Marx Brothers. And just try telling a knock-knock joke in Latin!

But we pay a price for poetry. English is not easy, as languages go. It began 1,500 years ago, when Germanic tribes (mainly Angles and Saxons) invaded Britain, a Celtic-speaking land already colonized by Latin-speaking Romans. Into this Anglo-Saxon stew went big dollops of French, Italian, Spanish, German, Danish, Portuguese, Dutch, Greek, and more Latin. Within a few hundred years, English was an extraordinarily rich broth. Today, it's believed to have the largest lexicon (that is, the most words) of any modern language—and it's still evolving. Is there any wonder the rules are a little screwy?

And let's face it, English *is* screwy. Bright, educated, technologically savvy people who can run a computer spreadsheet with their toes are heard every day saying things like:

"Come to lunch with the boss and I."

"Who forgot their umbrella?"

"Before the age of two, a mother's place is in the home."

Every one of those sentences has an outrageous howler (if you don't see them, check out chapters 1 and 7). Some kinds of flubs are becoming so common that they're starting to sound right to our ears. And in some cases, they are right. What used to be regarded as errors may now be acceptable or even preferred. What are we supposed to make of all this?

Woe Is I is a survival guide for intelligent people who probably never have diagrammed a sentence and never will. Most of us don't know a gerund from a gerbil and don't care, but we'd like to speak and write as though we did. Grammar is mysterious to each of us in a different way. Some very smart people mess up pronouns, and I've known brilliant souls who can't spell. Many people can't tell the difference between *it's* and *its*. Others go out of their way to avoid using quotation marks. Whatever your particular boo-boo, *Woe Is I* can help you fix it without hitting you over the head with a lot of technical jargon. No heavy lifting, no assembly required. There are sections on the worst pitfalls of everyday language, along with commonsense tips on how to avoid stumbling into them. Wherever possible, I've tried to stay away from grammatical terms, which most of us relish about as much as a vampire does garlic. You don't need them to use English well. If you come across a term that gives you trouble, there's a glossary in the back.

One last word before you plunge in. A dictionary is a wonderful tool, and everybody should have at least one. Yet the fact that a word can be found in the dictionary doesn't make it acceptable English. The job of a dictionary is to describe how words are used at a particular time. Formal or standard meanings are given, but so are colloquial, slang, dialect, substandard, regional, and other current meanings. A dictionary may tell you, for example, what's meant by words like "restauranteur" and "irregardless" (both, as you'll see, impostors)—but you wouldn't want to embarrass yourself by using them. Buy a standard dictionary (there are several recommended in the bibliography), and read the fine print.

The best of us sometimes get exasperated with the complexities of using English well. Believe me, it's worth the effort. Life might be easier if we all spoke Latin. But the quirks, the surprises, the ever-changing nature of English—these are the differences between a living language and a dead one.

Chapter 1

Woe Is I

Therapy for
Pronoun Anxiety

When a tiny word gives you a big headache, it's probably a pronoun.

Pronouns are usually small (*I, me, he, she, it*), but they're among the biggest troublemakers in the language. If you've ever been picked on by the pronoun police, don't despair. You're in good company. Hundreds of years after the first Ophelia cried "Woe is me," some pedants would argue that Shakespeare should have written "Woe is I" or "Woe is unto me." (Never mind that the rules of English grammar weren't even formalized in Shakespeare's day.) The point is that no one is exempt from having his pronouns second-guessed.

Put simply, a pronoun is an understudy for a noun. *He* may stand in for "Ralph," *she* for "Alice," *they* for "the Kramdens," and *it* for "the stuffed piranha." Why do we need them? Take the following sentence: *Ralph smuggled **his** stuffed piranha* *into the Kramdens' apartment, sneaked **it** out of **his** jacket, and was slipping **it** into **his** wife's curio cabinet, when suddenly Alice walked into **their** living room, clutched **her** heart, and screamed, "**You** get **that** out of **my** house!"*

If no one had invented pronouns, here's how that sentence would look: *Ralph smuggled Ralph's stuffed piranha into the Kramdens' apartment, sneaked the stuffed piranha out of Ralph's jacket, and was slipping the stuffed piranha into Ralph's wife's curio cabinet, when suddenly Alice walked into the Kramdens' living room, clutched Alice's heart, and screamed, "Ralph, get the stuffed piranha out of Alice's house!"*

See how much time pronouns save?

Simple substitutions (like *his* for *Ralph's*) are easy enough. Things get complicated when a pronoun, like any good understudy, takes on different guises, depending on the roles it plays in the sentence. Some pronouns are so well disguised that you may not be able to tell one from another. Enter: *that* and *which; it's* and *its; who's* and *whose; who* and *whom; everybody* and *nobody;* and *their, they're,* and *theirs.*

Now let's round up the usual suspects, as well as a few other shady characters.

The Which Trials: That or Which?

Bite on one of these: *Nobody likes a dog **that** bites* or *Nobody likes a dog **which** bites.*

If they both sound right, you've been spooked by *which*es (the first example is the correct one).

The old *that*-versus-*which* problem haunts everybody sooner or later. Here are two rules to help you figure out whether a clause (a group of words with its own subject and verb) should start with *that* or *which*.

- If you can drop the clause and not lose the point of the sentence, use *which*. If you can't, use *that*.
- A *which* clause goes inside commas. A *that* clause doesn't.

Now let's put the rules to work. Look at these two sentences:

*Buster's bulldog, **which** had one white ear, won best in show.*
*The dog **that** won best in show was Buster's bulldog.*

The point of each sentence is that Buster's dog won. What happens when we remove the *that* or *which* clause?

In the first example, the *which* clause (**which had one white ear**) is disposable—without it, we still have the gist of the sentence: *Buster's bulldog won best in show.*

But in the second example, the *that* clause (**that won best** *in show*) is essential. The sentence misses the point without it: *The dog was Buster's bulldog.*

Some people consider *which* more refined or elegant than *that.* Not so! In fact, *that* is more likely to be grammatically correct than *which.* That's because most of us don't put unessential information in the middle of our sentences, especially when speaking.

Here's a little memory aid:

C o m m a   S e n s e
Commas, *which* cut out the fat,
Go with *which,* never with *that.*

An Itsy-Bitsy Problem: It's or Its?

The smaller the word, the handier it is. And *it* is about as useful as they come. *It* can stand in for anything—a stuffed piranha, existentialism, the Monroe Doctrine, or buttered toast. It's a very versatile pronoun! But did you notice what just happened? We added an *s* and got *it's*—or should that be *its?* Hmmm. When do you use *it's,* and when do you use *its?*

This is an itsy-bitsy problem that gives lots of intelligent people fits. They go wrong when they assume a word with an apostrophe must be a possessive, like *Bertie's aunt.* But an apostrophe can also stand for something that's been omitted (as in contractions, which are run-together words like *can't* and *shouldn't*). In this case, *it's* is short for *it is*. Plain *its* is the possessive form. So here's the one and only rule you need:

- If you can substitute *it is,* use *it's.*

NOTE: *It's* can also be short for *it has.* There's more on *its* versus *it's* in the chapter on possessives, page 39.

Who's (or Whose) on First?

This problem is a first cousin of the one above (which you should look at, if you haven't already). As with *it's* and *its,* remember that *who's* is shorthand for *who is,* and unadorned *whose* is the possessive form.

- If you can substitute *who is,* use *who's.*

NOTE: *Who's* can also be short for *who has.* There's more on *whose* versus *who's* in the chapter on possessives, page 40.

You're on Your Own

"Your our kind of people," reads the hotel marquee. Eek! Let's hope impressionable children aren't looking. The sign should

Who's That?

Choose one: *The girl **that** married dear old dad* or *The girl **who** married dear old dad*.

If both sound right, it's because both are right.

A person can be either a *that* or a *who*. A thing, on the other hand, is always a *that*.

But what about Benjy and Morris? Dogs and cats aren't people, but they aren't quite things, either. Is an animal a *that* or a *who*?

If the animal is anonymous, or we don't use its name, it's a *that*: *There's the dog **that** won the Frisbee competition.*

If the animal has a name, he or she is a *who*: *Morris is a cat **who** knows what he likes.*

---

read: "You're our kind of people." *You're* is short for *you are*; *your* is the possessive form.

- If you can substitute *you are*, use *you're*.

Poor *whom*! Over the years, wordsmiths from Noah Webster to Jacques Barzun have suggested that maybe we should ditch it altogether and let *who* do the job of both. Not a bad idea. It's pretty hard to imagine an outraged populace protesting, "*Whom* do you think you're messing with! Get your hands off our pronouns!" There's no doubt that in everyday speech, *whom* has lost the battle.

So has the bell tolled for *whom*?

Not quite. Here we are, entering a new millennium, and against all odds, creaky old *whom* is still with us. With a few minor adjustments, we can get away with dropping it in our speech (I'll show you how in the box on page 9), though even that may raise an eyebrow or two. But since written English is more formal than conversational English, anyone who wants to write correctly will have to get a grip on *whom*.

If you want to be absolutely correct, the most important thing to know is that *who* does something (it's a subject, like *he*), and *whom* has something done to it (it's an object, like *him*). You might even try mentally substituting *he* or *him* where *who* or *whom* should go: if *him* fits, you want *whom* (both end in *m*); if *he* fits, you want *who* (both end in a vowel). *Who* does it *to* (*at, by, for, from, in, toward, upon, with*, etc.) *whom*. The words in parentheses, by the way, are prepositions, words that "position"—that is, locate—other words. A preposition often comes just before *whom*, but not always. A better way to decide between *who* and *whom* is to ask yourself *who* is doing what to *whom*.

This may take a little detective work. Miss Marple herself might have been stumped by the convolutions of some *who* or *whom* clauses (a clause, you'll recall, is a group of words with its own subject and verb). For instance, other words may get in between the subject and the verb. Or the object may end up in front of both the subject and the verb. Here are two pointers to help clear up the mystery, and examples of how they're used.

- Simplify, simplify, simplify: strip the clause down to its basic subject, verb, and object.
- Move the words around mentally to make it easier to identify the subject and the object.

*Nathan invited only guys [**who** or **whom**] he thought played for high stakes.* If you strip the clause of its false clues—the words separating the subject and verb—you end up with *who . . . played for high stakes. Who* did something (played for high stakes), so it's the subject.

*Nathan wouldn't tell Miss Adelaide [**who** or **whom**] he invited to his crap game.* First strip the sentence down to the basic clause, *[**who** or **whom**] he invited.* If it's still unclear, rearrange the words in your mind: *he invited **whom**.* You can now see that *whom* is the object—*he* did something to (invited) *whom*—even though *whom* comes ahead of both the verb and the subject.

N O T E : A preposition isn't necessarily followed by *whom.* It can be followed by a clause that starts with *who.* Consider this sentence: *After the crap game, Nathan was confused about [**who** or **whom**] owed him money.* Don't be misled by the preposition *about;* it's one of the

A Cure for the Whom-Sick

Now for the good news. In almost all cases, you can use *who* instead of *whom* in conversation or in informal writing, like personal letters and casual memos.

Sure, it's not a hundred percent correct, and I don't recommend using it on the most formal occasions, but *who* is certainly less stuffy, especially at the beginning of a sentence or a clause: **Who**'s *the letter from? Did I tell you* **who** *I saw at the movies?* **Who** *are you waiting to see? No matter* **who** *you invite, someone will be left out.*

A note of caution: *Who* can sound grating if used for *whom* right after a preposition. You can get around this by putting *who* in front. *From* **whom**? becomes **Who** *from?* So when a colleague tells you he's going on a Caribbean cruise and you ask, "Who with?" he's more likely to question your discretion than your grammar.

false clues mentioned above. Instead, simplify, simplify, simplify, and look for the clause—in this case it's **who owed him money**. Since *who* did something (owed him money), it's the subject.

Object Lessons

THE *ME* GENERATION

These days, anyone who says "It is I" sounds like a stuffed shirt. It wasn't always so. In bygone days, you might have had your knuckles rapped for saying "It's me" instead of "It is I." Your crime? A pronoun following the verb *to be,* the English teacher insisted, should act like a subject (*I, he, she, they*) and not an object (*me, him, her, them*). But language is a living thing, always evolving, and *It is I* is just about extinct. In all but the most formal writing, some of the fussiest grammarians accept *It's me.* Most of us find the old usage awkward, though I must admit that I still use "This is she" when someone asks for me on the phone. Old habits die harder than old rules.

Next time you identify the perp in a police lineup, feel free to point dramatically and say, "That's him, Officer!"

JUST BETWEEN *ME* AND *I*

Why is it that no one ever makes a mistake like this? *You'll be hearing from I.*

It's instinctive to use the correct form (*from **me***) when only a solitary pronoun comes after a preposition. (Prepositions—*after, as, at, before, between, by, for, from, in, like, on, toward, upon, with,* and a slew of others—position other words in the sentence.) But when the pronoun isn't alone, instinct goes down the drain, and grammar with it. So we run into abominations like *The odds were **against you and I***, although no one would dream of saying "against I."

I wouldn't be at all surprised to learn that the seeds of the *I*-versus-*me* problem are planted in early childhood. We're admonished to say, "I want a cookie," not "Me want a cookie." We begin to feel subconsciously that *I* is somehow more genteel than *me,* even in cases where *me* is the right choice—for instance, after a preposition.

My guess is that most people who make this mistake do so out of habit, without thinking, and not because they don't know the difference between *I* and *me.* If you find yourself automatically putting *you and I* after a preposition, try this: In your mind, put the tricky pronoun (*I* or *me*) first. You'll always choose the right one if it's first in line. Habits can be reversed—it's up to *me and you.*

> **NOTE:** I can hear a chorus of voices shouting, Wait a minute! Doesn't Shakespeare use *I* after a preposition in *The Merchant of Venice*? Antonio tells Bassanio, "All

debts are clear'd between you and I, if I might but see you at my death." That's true. But then, we're not Shakespeare.

More Than Meets the I

Some of the smartest people I know hesitate at the word *than* when it comes before a pronoun. What goes next, *I* or *me? he* or *him? she* or *her? they* or *them?*

The answer: All of the above! This is easier than it sounds. Take *I* and *me* as examples, since they're the pronouns we use most (egotists that we are). Either one may be correct after *than,* depending on the meaning of the sentence.

- *Trixie loves spaghetti **more than I*** means **more than I** *[do]*.
- *Trixie loves spaghetti **more than me*** means **more than** *[she loves]* **me**.

NOTE: If ending a sentence with *than I* or *than she* or *than they* seems awkward or fussy (particularly in speaking), you might simply add the missing thought: *Harry smokes more **than they do**.*

The Sins of the Self-ish

In the contest between *I* and *me*, the booby prize often goes to *myself*.

That's why we see sentences like *Jack and **myself** were married yesterday*. (It's *Jack and **I***.) Or like this more common *self*-promotion: *The project made money for Reynaldo and **myself***. The speaker isn't sure whether it's *Reynaldo and **me*** or *Reynaldo and **I***, so she goes with *Reynaldo and **myself***. Tsk, tsk. (It's *for Reynaldo and **me***.)

Myself and the rest of the *self*-ish crew (*yourself, himself, herself, itself, ourselves, yourselves, themselves*) shouldn't take the place of the ordinary pronouns *I* and *me, she* and *her,* and so on. They are used for only two purposes:

- To emphasize. *I made the cake **myself**. Love **itself** is a riddle. The detective **himself** was the murderer.* (The emphasis could be left out, and the sentence would still make sense.)
- To refer back to the subject. *She hates **herself**. And you call **yourself** a plumber! They consider **themselves** lucky to be alive. The problem practically solved **itself**.*

They and Company: They're, Their, Theirs (and There and There's)

These words remind me of the stateroom scene in the Marx Brothers movie *A Night at the Opera*. There seem to be half a dozen too many, all stepping on one another's feet.

Taken one at a time, though, they're pretty harmless.

- *They're* is shorthand for *they are*: **They're** *tightwads, and they always have been.*
- *Their* and *theirs* are the possessive forms for *they*: **Their** *money is* **theirs** *alone.*
- *There* (meaning "in or at that place," as opposed to "here") isn't even a pronoun, unlike the rest of the crowd in the stateroom. Neither is *there's*, which is shorthand for *there is*. But *there* and *there's* frequently get mixed up with the sound-alikes *they're, their,* and *theirs.*

Sometimes a limerick says it best:

The Dinner Guests

They seem to have taken on airs.
They're ever so rude with *their* stares.
They get *there* quite late,
There's a hand in your plate,
And *they're* eating what's not even *theirs.*

How Many Is Everybody?

What's wrong with saying, *Are everybody happy?* After all, when you use the word *everybody,* you're thinking of a crowd, right? Then why do we say, *Is everybody happy?* instead of *Are everybody happy?*

In other words, just how many people do we mean when we say *everybody* or *everyone?*

The answer is: one. Odd as it may seem, these pronouns are singular. We often use them when talking about whole gangs of people, but we treat them grammatically as individual gang members. The result is that each takes a singular verb: *Everybody **loves** a lover, but not everybody **is** one.*

There's No Their There

I'm not sure why, but many people start seeing double when they use *anybody, anyone, everybody, everyone, nobody, no one, somebody, someone, each, either,* and *neither.*

Actually, each of these pronouns is singular—yes, even *everybody* and *everyone* (if you have doubts, see the item above). Then why do so many people use the plurals *they, them, their,* and *theirs* as stand-ins? I cringe when I hear a sentence like *Somebody forgot to pay **their** bill.*

Stick to singular stand-ins for singular pronouns—*he, she, it, his, her, hers,* or *its: Somebody forgot to pay **his** bill.* You may be tempted to use *their* because you don't know whether the somebody is a he or a she. Well, your nonsexist intentions are good, but your grammar isn't. The pronouns *he* and *his* have been used since time immemorial to refer to people in general. If you can't bring yourself to use them, the somewhat awkward unisex alternatives are the compounds *he or she, his or her,* and *his or hers: Somebody forgot to pay **his or her** bill.* (Or, for that matter, you could forget the possessive: *Somebody forgot to pay the bill.*)

Here's how to use these pronouns. If they sound odd, it's probably because you're used to making mistakes. Join the club.

*Has **anybody** lost **her** purse?* Not: ***their** purse.*

*Anyone entering must show **his** ticket.* Not: ***their** ticket.*

***Everybody** has **his** priorities.* Not: ***their** priorities.*

***Everyone** seems happy with **his or her** partner.* Not: ***their** partner.*

***Nobody** truly knows **her** own mind.* Not: ***their** own mind.*

***No one** appreciates **her** husband.* Not: ***their** husband.*

***Somebody** must have **his** head screwed on backward.* Not: ***their** head.*

Someone** has locked **himself** out.* Not: ***themselves** or (even worse!) **themself.

***Each** has **its** drawbacks.* Not: ***their** drawbacks.*

***Either** has earned **his** stripes.* Not: ***their** stripes.*

***Neither** was wearing **his** earring.* Not: ***their** earring.*

NOTE: *Either* and *neither* can sometimes be plural when paired with *or* or *nor*. For more, see page 52.

What's What?

Which sentence is correct?

Lou sees **what appears** *to be ghosts* or *Lou sees* **what appear** *to be ghosts.*

Leaving aside the issue of Lou's sanity, should we choose *what appears* or *what appear?* And what difference does it make? Well, what we're really asking is whether the pronoun *what,* when used as a subject, takes a singular verb (*appears*) or a plural one (*appear*). The answer is that *what* can be either singular or plural; it can mean "the thing that" or "things that." In this case, Lou is seeing "things that" appear to be ghosts. So this is the correct sentence: *Lou sees* **what appear** *to be ghosts.*

NOTE: When *what* is the subject of two verbs in the same sentence, make the verbs match in number—both singular or both plural, not one of each. **What scares Lou the most is** *Bud's sudden disappearance.* (Both verbs are singular.) But **what seem** *to be supernatural events* **are** *really sleight-of-hand.* (Both verbs are plural.)

By the way, it takes a certain effort to get your *what*s straight. Few people do it automatically, so take your time and watch out for trapdoors. For more on *what* with verbs, see page 54.

Chapter 2

Plurals Before Swine

Blunders with Numbers

With grammar, it's always something. If it's not one thing, it's two—or four, or eight—and that's where plurals come in. Without plural words, we'd have to talk about one thing at a time! You couldn't eat a bag of *peanuts* at the ball game, you'd have to eat *peanut* after *peanut* after *peanut*. But language is very accommodating. A *bagful* here and a *bagful* there and— voilà—you've got *bagfuls*. See? There's nothing we can't have more of, even *infinities*, because anything that can be singular can also be plural.

What Noah Knew

The ark was filled symmetrically:
For every boy, a girl.
Its claim to singularity
Resided in the plural.

In English, it's fairly easy to go forth and multiply. To make a singular noun (a word for a thing, person, place, or idea) into a plural one, we usually add *s* or *es* or *ies,* depending on its ending. In general, plurals are a piece (or pieces) of cake.

Of course, there are dozens of irregular plurals, but most of them are second nature to us by the time we're five or six. *Children* (not "childs") shouldn't play with *knives* (not "knifes"), and ganders are male *geese* (not "gooses"). A little later in life we pick up some of the more exotic kinds of plurals—*criteria, phenomena, tableaux,* and the like—that are the offspring of other languages.

For most of us, plurals get sticky mainly when they involve proper names, nouns with several parts, or words that can be either singular or plural. How do we refer to more than one *Sanchez* or *spoonful* or *brother-in-law*? Is a word like *couple* or *politics* singular or plural—or can it be both?

To get right to the points, let's start with names.

Keeping Up
with the Joneses:
How Names Multiply

It baffles me why people mangle names almost beyond recognition when they make them plural. *In my daughter's preschool class, there are two **Larries** [ouch!], three **Jennifer's** [oof!], and two **Sanchez'** [yech!].* It's *Larrys, Jennifers,* and *Sanchezes.*

Getting it right isn't that difficult. Whether you're dealing with a first name or a last, form the plural by adding s, or (if the name ends in s, sh, ch, x, or z) by adding es. A final y doesn't change to ies at the end of a name. And please, no apostrophes!

*Charles and his friend Charles are just a couple of **Charleses**.*

*When Eliza dated three guys named Henry, she couldn't keep her **Henrys** straight. What's more, two of them were **Higginses**.*

*There are eight **Joneses**, two of them **Marys**, in Reggie's little black book.*

*The **Ricardos** and the **Mertzes** had dinner with the **Simpsons** and the **Flanderses** at the home of the **Cleavers**.*

Compound Fractures: Words That Come Apart

Some nouns aren't simple; they're more like small construction projects. When a *spoon* is *full*, it's a *spoonful*—but are two of them *spoonsful* or *spoonfuls*? If your better half has two brothers, are they your *brothers-in-law* or your *brother-in-laws*? In other words, how do you make a plural of a noun with several parts? The answer, as it turns out, comes in parts:

- If a compound word is solid and has no hyphen (-), add the normal plural ending to the *end* of the word:

  Churchmen love **soapboxes**.

  Kipling appeals to **schoolchildren** *and* **fishwives**.

  Doormen *are good at getting* **taxicabs**.

  You hardly ever come across Biedermeier **bookcases** *in alleyways*.

  Babies dump **spoonfuls** *of jam on* **footstools**.

- If the word is split into parts, with or without hyphens, add the plural ending to the root or most important part (underlined in the examples):

  Mothers-in-law *like to attend* **courts-martial**.

  Are they **ladies-in-waiting** *or just* **hangers-on**?

  Those **counselors-at-law** *ate all the* **crêpes** *suzette*.

- Watch out for *general* when it's part of a compound word. In a military title, *general* is usually the important part, so it gets the *s*. In a civilian title, *general* isn't the root, so it doesn't get the *s*:

> Two <u>attorneys</u> general *went dancing with two* **major** <u>generals</u>.
>
> *Those* <u>consuls</u> general *are retired* **brigadier** <u>generals</u>.

The ics Files

Figuring out the mathematics of a noun can be tricky. Take the word *mathematics*. Is it singular or plural? And what about all those other words ending in *ics—economics, ethics, optics, politics,* and so on? Fortunately, it doesn't take a Ph.D. in mathematics to solve this puzzle.

If you're using an *ics* word in a general way (as a branch of study, say), it's singular. If you're using an *ics* word in a particular way (as someone's set of beliefs, for example), it's plural.

> "**Politics** *stinks,*" *said Sonny.*
>
> "*Sonny's* **politics** *stink,*" *said Gopher.*
>
> **Statistics** *isn't a very popular course.*
>
> *The company's* **statistics** *are often misleading.*

Ifs, Ands, or Buts

In English, there are exceptions to every rule. When *man* or *woman* is part of a compound, often both parts become plural. For example, *man-servant* becomes *menservants; woman doctor* becomes *women doctors; gentleman farmer* becomes *gentlemen farmers.* Two other exceptions to the rules for making compound words plural make no sense at all: *hotfoot* becomes *hotfoots* (believe it or not), and *still life* becomes *still lifes.* Go figure.

On occasion you may need to form a plural of a word like *yes, no,* or *maybe.* Well, since you're referring to them as nouns, just follow the normal rules for making nouns into plurals:

WORDS TO THE WHYS

Ups and downs and ins and outs,
Forevers and nevers and whys.
Befores and afters, dos and don'ts,
Farewells and hellos and good-byes.
Life is a string of perhapses,
A medley of whens and so whats.
We rise on our yeses and maybes,
Then fall on our nos and our buts.

Two-Faced Words:
Sometimes Singular,
Sometimes Plural

A noun can be double trouble if it stands for a collection of things. Sometimes it's singular and sometimes it's plural. How do you know which is which? Amazingly, common sense (yes, it does have a place in English usage!) should tell you. Ask yourself this question: Am I thinking of the baseball team, or the players? Let's take a swing at these problem words a few at a time.

COUNSELING FOR COUPLES

What is a *couple,* anyway? Is it a pair (singular), or two of a kind (plural)? Is it two peas (plural) in a pod, or a pod (singular) with two peas?

Couple is probably the most common of the two-faced words. It can be either singular or plural, depending on whether it's supposed to mean two individuals or a package deal. Ask yourself whether you have the two peas in mind, or the pod. Here's a hint: Look at the word (*a* or *the*) in front. *The couple* is usually singular. *A couple,* especially when followed by *of,* is usually plural. Each of these examples illustrates both (the verbs are underlined, one plural and one singular):

*A **couple** of tenants <u>own</u> geckos. The **couple** in 5G <u>owns</u> a ferret.*

*Only a **couple** of appointments are available. That **couple** is always late.*

There's more about *couple* in the chapter on verbs; see page 53.

GROUP THERAPY

Many words that mean a group of things—*total, majority,* and *number,* for example—can be singular or plural. Sometimes they mean the group acting as a whole, sometimes the members of the group.

As with the other two-faced words, ask yourself whether you are thinking of the whole or the parts. A little hint: *The* before the word (*the total, the majority*) is usually a tip-off that it's singular, while *a* (*a total, a number*), especially when *of* comes after, usually indicates a plural. Each of these examples illustrates both (the verbs are underlined, one singular and one plural):

*The **majority** is in charge. Still, a **majority** of voters are unhappy.*

*The **total** was in the millions. A **total** of six were missing.*

*The **number** of hats Bette owns is astounding. A **number** of them are pretty ridiculous.*

There's more about *total, majority,* and *number* in the chapter on verbs, page 53.

ALL OR NOTHING

All is a very versatile word. It's all things to all people; in fact, it's all-encompassing. So all-inclusive is this little word that it can be either singular or plural. Another two-faced word!

Luckily, it's all too simple to decide whether *all* is singular or plural. Here's a foolproof way (the verbs in the examples are underlined):

- If *all* means "all of it" or "everything" or "the only thing," it's singular: "**All** I eat <u>is</u> lettuce," said Kate. "But **all** I lose <u>is</u> brain cells. **All** <u>is</u> not well with my waist."
- If *all* indicates "all of them," it's plural. "**All** the men I date <u>are</u> confused," said Kate. "**All** <u>prefer</u> slender women with big appetites."

NOTE: The same logic holds for *any.* If it means "any of it," it's singular; if it means "any of them," it's plural. There's more about *any* and *all* in the chapter on verbs, page 53.

NONE SENSE

None is the most difficult of the two-faced words, those that can be either singular or plural. One reason it's so confusing is that generations of us were taught (incorrectly) as school-children that *none* is always singular because it means "not one." Legions of people think of rather stiff sentences—**None** of Dempsey's teeth <u>was</u> chipped, or **None** of Tunney's fingers <u>was</u> broken—as grammatically correct.

But *none* has always been closer in meaning to "not any," and most authorities agree it's usually plural: ***None** of Tyson's teeth <u>were</u> chipped.* ***None** of Holyfield's fingers <u>were</u> broken. None* is singular only when it means "none of it" (that is to say, "no amount"): ***None** of the referee's blood <u>was</u> shed.*

Here's an easy way to decide whether *none* is singular or plural (the verbs are underlined):

- If it suggests "none of them," it's plural: ***None** of the fans <u>are</u> fighting.* ***None** <u>are</u> excited enough.*
- If it means "none of it," it's singular: ***None** of the bout <u>was</u> seen in Pittsburgh.* ***None** <u>was</u> worth broadcasting.*

  NOTE: When you really do mean "not one," it's better to say "not one," and use a singular verb: ***Not one** of Holyfield's fingers <u>was</u> broken.*

Y's and Wherefores: Words That End in Y

Some plurals are just a bowl of cherries. Words ending in *y* either add *s* or change the *y* to *ies*. Here's the scoop.

- If a word ends in *y* preceded by a consonant (a hard sound), like *b, d, l, r, t,* etc., drop the *y* and add *ies:* ***Ladies** don't throw **panties** off the decks of **ferries.***

● If a word ends in *y* preceded by a vowel (a soft, open-mouthed sound, like *a, e, o, u*), add *s*: **Boys born in alleys can grow up to be attorneys**.

For making plurals out of names that end in *y*, see page 21.

One Potato, Two Potato: Words That End in O

O for a simple solution to this one! Unfortunately, there's no hard-and-fast rule that tells you how to form the plural of every word that ends in *o*.

● Most form their plurals by adding *s*: **Romeos** *who wear* **tattoos** *and invite* **bimbos** *to their* **studios** *to see their* **portfolios** *are likely to be* **gigolos**.

● A small number of words that end in *o* form their plurals by adding *es*. Some of the most common are in this example: The **heroes** *saved the* **cargoes** *of* **tomatoes** *and* **potatoes** *from the* **mosquitoes** *and* **tornadoes** *by hiding them in* **grottoes**.

If you're unsure about the plural of an *o* word, look it up in the dictionary. And if two plurals are given, the one that's listed first is the preferred spelling.

Plurals on the Q.T.:
Abbreviations, Letters,
and Numbers

No two authorities seem to agree on how we should form the plurals of abbreviations (*GI, r.p.m.*), letters (*x, y, z*), and numbers (*9, 10*). Should we add *s*, or *'s*? Where one style maven sees *UFO's*, another sees *UFOs*. One is nostalgic for the *1950's*, the other for the *1950s*. This is more a matter of taste and readability than of grammar, and frankly, we have better things to worry about. For the sake of consistency and common sense, here's what I recommend. To form the plurals of all numbers, letters, and abbreviations (with or without periods and capitals), simply add *'s*.

CPA's, those folks who can add columns of 9's in their heads, have been advising M.D.'s since the 1980's to mind their p's and q's, and never to accept IOU's. Things could be worse: there could be two IRS's.

Between and From:
The Numbers Game

OK, it's not something that's been keeping you awake nights. But it comes up all the time. The question: When a noun follows *between* or *from,* is it singular or plural? *The elevator* stalled **between** the ninth and tenth [*floor* or *floors*], *stranding the boss* **from** *the first to the third [week or weeks] in August.* See what I mean? A small problem, perhaps, but a common one.

The answer: *Between* is followed by a plural noun, and *from* is followed by a singular one: *The elevator stalled* **between** *the ninth and tenth* **floors,** *stranding the boss* **from** *the first to the third* **week** *in August.*

Another pair of examples:

Veronica said she lost her charm bracelet somewhere **between** *Thirty-third and Thirty-seventh* **streets.** *Archie searched every inch of pavement* **from** *Thirty-third to Thirty-seventh* **Street** *before realizing that she had been in a cab at the time.*

The Soul of Kindness: All Kinds, Sorts, and Types

You've probably heard sentences like this one: *I hate* **these kind** *of mistakes!* If it sounds wrong to you, you're right. It's **these kinds** *of mistakes (or* **that kind** *of mistake).*

The singulars—*kind* of, *sort* of, *type* of, and *style* of—are preceded by *this* or *that,* and are followed by singular nouns: *Dagwood wears* **this kind of hat.**

The plurals—*kinds* of, *sorts* of, *types* of, and *styles* of—are preceded by *these* or *those,* and are usually followed by plural nouns: *Mr. Dithers hates* **those kinds of hats.**

Here are some more examples to help you sort things out:

*"I enjoy **this sort of cigar**," said Dagwood.*

*"**These sorts of cigars** disgust me," said Mr. Dithers.*

*"**That type of car** is my ideal," said Dagwood.*

*"Only gangsters drive **those types of cars**," said Mr. Dithers.*

Never use *a* or *an* after the expressions *kind of, sort of, type of,* or *variety of: The beagle is a **kind of a** hound.* (Ugh!)

> **NOTE:** Some singular nouns can stand for just one thing (*Is the **meat** ready?*) or a whole class of things (*The butcher sells many varieties of **meat***). Other singular nouns always stand for a set of things (*The **china** matches the **furniture***). When a singular noun stands for a group of things, it's all right (though not necessary) to use it with *those kinds, these sorts,* and so on. ***Those kinds of china** break easily.* This can be a subtle distinction. If you find it hard to make, you're safer sticking to the all-singular or all-plural rule (*this kind of china*).

Some Things Never Change

You're already familiar with nouns from the animal kingdom that can stand for one critter or many: *fish, deer, moose, vermin, elk, sheep, swine.* Well, some words ending in *s* are also the same in singular and plural: *series, species,* and *headquar-*

ters, which can mean a base or bases: *Gizmo's **headquarters** was designed by Rube Goldberg. The rival companies' **headquarters** were on opposite sides of town.*

Looks Can Be Deceiving

Loads of nouns look plural because they end in *s*, but they're actually singular: *checkers* (also *billiards, dominoes,* and other names of games); *measles* (also *mumps, rickets, shingles,* and many other diseases); *molasses; news;* and *whereabouts. Basil says **checkers** takes Sybil's mind off her **shingles**, which is driving her nuts.*

If that's not confusing enough, how about this? Some nouns that end in *s* and are regarded as pairs—*scissors, trousers, tongs, pliers, tweezers,* and *breeches,* for instance—are singular but treated as plural. *The **scissors** were found, as were the **tweezers**, in the drawer where the **pliers** are kept.*

> **NOTE:** Some words are frequently used as singular (*media, data*), although the traditional meaning is plural. The ground is shifting here, so for the scoop on *data* and *media*, see page 183. And if you want a little thrill—all right, I said a *little* thrill—look up *kudos* (singular or plural?) on page 111.

Plurals
with Foreign Accents

A Californian I know, Dr. Schwartz, is a cactus fancier. Is his garden filled with *cactuses* . . . or *cacti*?

As most dictionaries will tell you, either form is right. *Cacti* may sound more exotic, but it's not more correct; in fact, many American dictionaries favor *cactuses*.

As for other nouns of foreign origin, how do you know whether to choose an Anglicized plural (like *memorandums*) or a foreign one (*memoranda*)? There's no single answer, unfortunately. A century ago, the foreign ending would have been preferred, but over the years we've given Anglicized plural endings to more and more foreign-derived words. When you have a choice, take the plural that's listed first in the dictionary.

Here's a partial list of current preferences.

Anglicized: *antennas* (except those on insects), *appendixes*, *cactuses, curriculums, dictums, formulas, gymnasiums, indexes, memorandums, millenniums, referendums, stadiums, symposiums, ultimatums, virtuosos.*

Multiple Mollusks
In the oceans, wriggling by,
Are *octopuses*, not *octopi*.

Foreign: *analyses, antennae* (on insects), *addenda, algae, axes* (for *axis*), *bacteria, bases* (for *basis*), *beaux, châteaux* (*châteaus* is gaining fast), *crises, criteria, fungi, hypotheses, kibbutzim, larvae, oases, parentheses, phenomena, radii* (but *radiuses* is on the rise), *stimuli, strata, tableaux* (*tableaus* is catching up), *theses, vertebrae.*

Chapter 3

Yours Truly

The Possessives and the Possessed

For an acquisitive society, we're awfully careless about possessives. Have you ever driven through a vacation community and noticed the offhanded signs identifying the properties? *The Miller's, The Davis', The Jone's, Bobs Place.* Businesses are no better, imagining possessives where there aren't any. A theater near Times Square in New York declares itself *The Ero's.* We've all seen places like *Harrys Muffler Shop* or *Glorias' House of Beauty* or *His' and Hers' Formal Wear.*

The word *its* is an Excedrin headache, a possessive that does not take the apostrophe (') we've come to expect. There are scores of other possessive puzzles: Are you a friend *of Jake,* or a friend *of Jake's*? Are you going to your *aunt and uncle's* house, or to your *aunt's and uncle's* house? Do you mind *me smoking,* or do you mind *my smoking*?

As long as there are haves and have-nots, there will be questions about possessives. This chapter should answer the most troublesome ones.

Possession Is Not Demonic: The Simple Facts

The tool kit couldn't be simpler. All you need to make almost any word possessive is an apostrophe and the letter *s*. You add both of them together ('*s*) or just the apostrophe alone, depending on the circumstances:

- If the word is singular, always add '*s*, regardless of its ending. (This is true even if the ending is *s*, *z*, or *x*— whether sounded or silent.) *The waiter spilled red wine on **Demi's** dress, which came from **Kansas's** finest shop. The **dress's** skirt, which resembled a tutu from one of **Degas's** paintings, was ruined. **Bruce's** attitude was philosophical because he had been reading **Camus's** essays. "It wasn't **Jacques's** fault," he said, defending the waiter. "Besides, this isn't that **Bordeaux's** best vintage."*

- If the word is plural and doesn't already end in *s*, add '*s*: *The **children's** menu was a rip-off, and the **men's** room was painted fuchsia.*

- If the word is plural and ends in *s*, add just the apostrophe: *The **Willises'** car was stolen by the valet parking* attendant. *The **cops'** attitude was surly. The **victims'** evening was now demolished.*

And by the way, when you need a comma or a period after a possessive word that ends with an apostrophe, the comma or period goes after the apostrophe and not inside it: *The idea was the **girls'**, or maybe the **boys'**, but at any rate the responsibility was their **parents'**.*

> **NOTE:** Be sure you've formed the plural correctly before you add the apostrophe to the end. There's more about plural names in the chapter on plurals, page 21. In a nutshell, if a name ends in *s* (like *Willis*) the plural adds *es* (the *Willises*) and the plural possessive adds *es'* (the *Willises'* car). For a name that doesn't end in an *s* sound (*Babbitt*), the plural adds *s* (the *Babbitts*) and the plural possessive adds *s'* (the *Babbitts'* car).

Its (or It's?): Public Enemy Number 1

What a difference an apostrophe makes. Every possessive has one, right? Well, not necessarily so. *It* (like *he* and *she*) is a pronoun—a stand-in for a noun—and pronouns don't have apostrophes when they're possessives: ***His** coat is too loud because of **its** color, but **hers** is too mousy.*

Now, as for *it's* (the one with the punctuation), the apostrophe stands for something that has been removed. *It's* is short for *it is,* and the apostrophe replaces the missing *i* in *is.* *The parakeet is screeching because **it's** time to feed him.*

Here's how to keep *its* and *it's* straight:

● If the word you want could be replaced by *it is,* you want *it's.* If not, use *its.* (There's more on *its* and *it's* in the chapter on pronouns, page 4.)

N O T E : Sometimes *it's* can be short for *it has,* as in: ***It's** been hours since he ate.*

✳ **W h o ' s   W h o s e ?** ✳

The battle between *whose* and *who's* comes up less frequently than the one between *its* and *it's* (see above), but the problems are identical. If you can solve one, you've got the other one whipped.

Don't be misled by the apostrophe. Not every possessive has one. *Who* (like *it* and *he*) is a pronoun—a stand-in for a noun—and pronouns don't have apostrophes when they're possessives: *"**Whose** frog is this?" said Miss Grundy.*

Now, as for *who's,* the apostrophe stands for something that has been removed. *Who's* is short for *who is,* and the apostrophe replaces the missing *i* in *is.* *"And **who's** responsible for putting it in my desk?"*

Here's how to keep *whose* and *who's* straight:

• If you can substitute *who is*, use *who's*. If not, use *whose*.

NOTE: Sometimes *who's* can be short for *who has*, as in: **Who's had lunch?**

Their Is But to Do or Die

His newest book, Monster Truck, *is written especially for the child with machinery on* **their** *mind.* Hmm . . . *their*? Let's hope this children's book is better written than the ad.

Their, the possessive form of *they,* is often used mistakenly for *his* or *her,* as in: **No one in their right mind pays retail.** Ouch! *No one* is singular, and the possessive that goes with it should be singular, too: **No one in her right mind pays retail.**

I suspect many people are reluctant to use *his* or *her* when they aren't referring to anyone in particular. But until our language has a sex-neutral possessive to use instead, we are stuck with *his,* or *her,* or the clumsy compound *his or her.* To substitute *their* may be politically correct, but it's grammatically impaired.

For problems with *their* and its sound-alikes, see the chapter on pronouns, page 14.

Group Ownership: When Possessives Come in Pairs

If something has two owners, who really owns it? If two people share an experience, whose experience is it? Who, in other words, gets the apostrophe when Sam and Janet spend an evening out—is it *Sam and Janet's evening,* or *Sam's and Janet's evening?*

- If two people (*Sam and Janet*) possess something (an *evening*) in common, consider them a single unit and put a single *'s* at the end: ***Sam and Janet's** evening was ruined when their date ended at the police station.*
- If two people possess something (or some things) individually, rather than jointly, each name gets an *'s*: ***Sam's and Janet's** furniture—his Danish modern, her French rococo—would never work in the same apartment.* Or ***Sam's and Janet's** couches came from the same store.*
- If the names of the two owners are replaced by pronouns (stand-ins for nouns, like *your, my, our,* etc.), don't use them side by side, as in *"**Your and my** furniture can't live together," said Janet.* It sounds better with the noun in between: *"**Your** furniture and **mine** can't live together."*

Nobody's Fool

Body language is no problem in the possessive. Words like *anybody, everybody, somebody,* and *nobody* become possessive when you add *'s: anybody's, everybody's, somebody's, nobody's.*

When *else* is added, the *'s* goes after *else*: "Archie is mine, and **nobody else's,**" said Betty. This seems pretty obvious to us now, but there was a time when it was considered correct to leave the apostrophe with the pronoun: *Is that your suit of armor, Sir Lancelot, or* **somebody's else?**

For Goodness' Sake!

Some word formations are just too much for us to get our tongues around. That's the only good reason I can think of for this next exception to the usual rules on possessives.

We may do something for *pity's* sake, for *heaven's* sake, for the *nation's* sake, for our *children's* sake. But some of the "sake" phrases—for *goodness'* sake, for *conscience'* sake, for *appearance'* sake, for *righteousness'* sake—don't take the final *s* that normally follows the apostrophe. Call it tradition. I suppose our English-speaking forebears decided there was enough hissing in those words already, without adding another sibilant syllable (say those last two words five times in rapid succession).

It's often customary to drop the final *s* when forming the possessives of ancient classical names that already end in *s*: *Whose biceps were bigger,* **Hercules'** *or* **Achilles'**?

A r e   Y o u   T o o   P o s s e s s i v e ?

One way to make a noun possessive is to add *'s*; another way is to put *of* in front of it.

What about using both? Are two possessives better than one? Should we say *a friend* **of Jake**? Or *a friend* **of Jake's**? I'll end the suspense quickly. Both are correct.

But when a pronoun is involved, make it a possessive: *a friend of* **his,** not *a friend of* **him**: *Jake is a guest of my* **daughter** [or **daughter's**], *which makes him a guest of* **mine**.

D o i n g   T i m e

Time is money, they say, and both are valuable, which may be why they're sometimes expressed in a possessive way. It's long been the custom in English that we may, if we wish, describe periods of time and amounts of money by using possessives: *After an* **hour's** *wait in court, Butch was given* **two years'** *pro-*

bation for stealing **fifty dollars'** worth of change from the collection plate.

Of course, you can say the same thing without using any possessives: *After waiting an hour in court, Butch was given two years of probation for stealing fifty dollars in change from the collection plate.*

Do You Mind Me . . . Uh . . . My Smoking?

For many of us, this one is the Gordian knot of possessive puzzles. Actually, it's not hard to untie, once you know the secret. First, let's see how you do on your own. Which is correct?

1. *He resents **my going**.*
2. *He resents **me going**.*

If you picked number 2, you goofed, but don't beat up on yourself. You're a member of a large and distinguished club. To see why so many of us slip up, let's look at two similar examples:

1. *He resents **my departure**.*
2. *He resents **me departure**.*

I'll bet you didn't have any trouble with that one. Obviously, number 1 is correct. *Departure* is a noun (a thing), and when it is modified or described by a pronoun (a word that stands in for a noun), the pronoun has to be a possessive: *my, his, her, your,* and so on.

Now look again at the first set of examples:

1. *He resents **my going**.*
2. *He resents **me going**.*

If you still feel like picking number 2, it's because *ing* words are chameleons. They come from verbs—*go,* in the case of *going*—and usually act like verbs. But every once in a while they step out of character and take on the role of nouns. For all intents and purposes they may as well be nouns; in this example, *going* may as well be the noun *departure*.

The $64,000 question: How do we figure out whether an *ing* word is acting like a verb or like a noun? Here's a hint: If you can substitute a noun for the *ing* word—*departure* in place of *going,* for example, or *habit* for *smoking*—then treat it like a noun. That means making the word in front a possessive (*my,* not *me*): *He can't stand **my smoking**.*

Loose Ends

The preceding explanation unties the Gordian knot, and you can stop there if you want. But there are a couple of loose ends you may want to finish off.

Sometimes it's too clumsy to use a possessive along with an *ing* word—for instance, when you'd have to make a whole slew of words possessive, and not just one. Here's an example: *Basil objects to* **men and women kissing** *in public.* Using the possessive (*men's and women's kissing*) would create a monster. It's good to follow a rule, except when it leads you off a cliff. Since there's no way to mistake the meaning, leave it alone. But if there's just a pronoun in front, stick to the rule and make it a possessive: *Basil objects to* **our kissing** *in public.* (Not: *Basil objects to* **us kissing** *in public.*)

Another complication is the kind of sentence that can go either way:

Basil dislikes that **woman's wearing** *shorts.*

Basil dislikes that **woman wearing** *shorts.*

Both are correct, but they mean different things. In the first example, Basil dislikes shorts on the woman. In the second, he dislikes the woman herself. The lesson? Lighten up, Basil!

Chapter 4

They Beg to Disagree

Putting Verbs in Their Place

The verb is the business end of a sentence, the sentence's reason for being. That's where the action is. Without a verb, even if it's only suggested, there's nothing going on, just a lot of nouns standing around with their hands in their pockets. A verb is easy to spot. Just look for the moving target, the center of activity, the part that tells you what's going on. No wonder the verb is often the most interesting word in a sentence.

It's also the most complicated. Because a verb expresses action, it has a dimension that other words lack—time. It has to tell you whether something happened in the past, the present, the future, or some combination of times: *sneeze, sneezed, will sneeze, would have sneezed,* and so on. The verb has another dimension, too. It varies according to the subject (who or what is performing the action): *I sneeze, he sneezes, they sneeze,* and so on.

There are plenty of reasons a verb can go astray. The most common is that it doesn't match the subject: one is singular and the other plural (*Harry and I **was sneezing**,* for example). The next most common reason is that the verb's timing—its tense—is off (*Yesterday she **sneezes***).

Then there are those pesky little verbs that are as annoying as ants at a picnic, and just about as hard to tell apart: *sit* and *set, rise* and *raise, lie* and *lay.*

This makes verbs sound daunting, but they're really not so bad. Taken one at a time (which is how you encounter them, after all), problems with verbs can be made to disappear.

Making Verbs Agreeable

Some rules of grammar shift every generation or so, but you can bet the bank that this one will never change: Subject and verb must agree. If the subject is singular, so is the verb (*Ollie stumbles*). If the subject is plural, so is the verb (*Stan and Ollie stumble*).

If your verb (the action word) doesn't match its subject (who or what is doing the action), you probably have the wrong subject in mind. That's not unusual, since the real subject isn't always easy to see. If you find it a breeze to write a simple sentence, but start hyperventilating when a few bells and whistles are added, you're not alone. Here's what I mean:

*Every part of Ollie **needs** a massage.*

No problem. The subject (*part*) is singular, so the verb (*needs*) is singular. Now let's add a few of Ollie's aching parts:

*Every part of Ollie—his legs, his neck, his shoulders, his feet—[**needs** or **need**] a massage.*

Since the closest word is *feet,* a plural, you might be tempted to pick *need.* But in fact, the verb stays the same, *needs,* despite the added details. That's because the subject itself (*part*) hasn't changed. The key to making subject and verb agree is to correctly identify the subject, and for that you have to simplify the sentence in your mind and eliminate the extraneous stuff. Here are a couple of tips on simplifying a sentence:

- Extra information inserted between subject and verb doesn't alter the verb.

  *Spring's glory **was** lost on Ollie.*

  *Spring's glory, with its birds and its flowers and its trees, **was** lost on Ollie.*

  The subject, *glory,* is still singular, no matter how much information you add to it.

- Phrases such as *along with, as well as, in addition to,* and *together with,* inserted between subject and verb, don't alter the verb.

  *Spring **was** a tonic for Stan.*

*Spring, along with a few occasional flirtations, **was** a tonic for Stan.*

The subject is still *spring,* and is singular.

• Descriptions (adjectives) added to the subject don't alter the verb.

*A substance **was** stuck to Stan's shoe.*

*A green, slimy, and foul-smelling substance **was** stuck to Stan's shoe.*

The subject is *substance,* and it stays singular no matter how many disgusting adjectives you pile on.

SPLIT DECISIONS

Often the subject of a sentence—whoever or whatever is doing the action—is a two-headed creature with *or* or *nor* in the middle: **Milk or cream** *is fine, thank you.*

When both halves of the subject—the parts on either side of *or* or *nor*—are singular, so is the verb: *Neither alcohol nor tobacco **is** allowed.* When both halves are plural, so is the verb: *Ties or cravats **are** required.*

But how about when one half is singular and the other plural? Do you choose a singular or a plural verb? *Neither the eggs nor the milk [**was** or **were**] fresh.*

The answer is simple. If the subject nearer the verb is singular, the verb is singular: *Neither the eggs nor the **milk was** fresh.* If the subject nearer the verb is plural, the verb is plural: *Neither the milk nor the **eggs were** fresh.*

The same rule applies when subjects are paired with *not only* and *but also: Not only the chairs but also the **table was** sold.* Or: *Not only the table but also the **chairs were** sold.*

THE SUBJECT WITH MULTIPLE PERSONALITIES

Say you've identified the subject of a sentence, and it's a word that could be interpreted as either singular or plural, like *couple, total, majority, number, any, all,* or *none.* Is the verb singular or plural?

Here's how to decide.

Words that stand for a group of things—*couple, total, majority,* and *number*—sometimes mean the group as a whole (singular), and sometimes mean the individual members of the group (plural). The presence of *the* before the word (*the couple, the total, the majority*) is often a clue that it's singular, so use a singular verb: ***The couple lives** in apartment 9A.* When *a* comes before the word, and especially when *of* comes after (*a couple of, a number of*), it's probably plural, so use a plural verb: ***A couple of** deadbeats **live** in apartment 9A.*

The words *all, any,* and *none* can also be either singular or plural. If you're using them to suggest *all of it, any of it,* or *none of it,* use a singular verb: ***All** the money [all of it] **is** spent.* If you're suggesting *all of them, any of them,* or *none of them,* use a plural verb: ***All** the customers [all of them] **are** gone.*

There's more about these two-edged words in the chapter on plurals, pages 25–28.

What and Whatnot

Here's another multiple personality—a word that can be either singular or plural. Take a look at these examples:

What is *going on here?* **What are** *your intentions, Buster?*

As you can see, *what* can be either singular or plural when it's the subject of a verb. If *what* stands for one thing, use a singular verb (*is,* in this case). If it stands for several things, use a plural verb (*are,* for example).

But how do you choose? Consider this sentence: *Phyllis is wearing* **what** *[look or looks] like false eyelashes.* Just ask yourself whether *what* refers to "a thing that" or "things that." In this case, she is wearing *things* that *look* like false eyelashes. Use the plural verb: *Phyllis is wearing* **what look** *like false eyelashes.*

> **NOTE:** When *what* affects two verbs in the same sentence, the verbs should be alike—both singular or both plural, not one of each: **What gives** *away Phyllis's age* **is** *her bad knees.* In other words, the thing about Phyllis that gives away her age is the fact that she has bad knees. On the other hand, if you want to emphasize that both of Phyllis's knees have gone bad, you should choose plurals for both verbs: **What give** *away Phyllis's age* **are** *her two bad knees.* As you may suspect, there can be room for disagreement about whether *what* should be singular or plural. The important thing to remember is that if *what* affects two verbs, they should match—both singular or both plural.

There's more about *what* in the chapter on pronouns; see page 17.

THERE, THERE, NOW!

When a statement starts with *there,* the verb can be either singular or plural. We can say *there is* or *there are.* Just look for the subject of the sentence, which in this case follows the verb instead of coming before it.

"**There is** *a fly in my soup!*" said Mr. LaFong. "*And* **there are** *lumps in the gravy!*"

In the first example, the subject is *fly;* in the second, it's *lumps.* If the subject is hard for you to see, just delete *there* in your mind and turn the statement around: "*A* *fly* **is** *in my soup! And lumps* **are** *in the gravy!*"

For more on *there* at the head of a sentence, see page 184.

Wishful Thinking: I Wish I Was . . . or . . . I Wish I Were?

"Difficult do you call it, Sir?" the lexicographer Samuel Johnson once said after hearing a violinist perform. "I wish it were impossible."

Were? Why not *I wish it* **was** *impossible?* Well, in English we have a special way of speaking wishfully. We say, *I wish I* *were in love again,* not *I wish I **was** in love again.* There's a peculiar, wishful kind of grammar for talking about things that are desirable, as opposed to things as they really are. When we're in a wishful mood (a grammarian would call it the subjunctive mood), *was* becomes *were*:

*I wish I **were** in Paris.* (I'm not in Paris.)

*They wish he **weren't** so obnoxious.* (He is so obnoxious.)

*She wishes New York **were** cleaner.* (New York isn't cleaner.)

*He wishes Julia **were** home more often.* (Julia isn't home more often.)

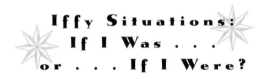

Iffy Situations: If I Was . . . or . . . If I Were?

What a difference an *if* makes. An ordinary, straightforward statement like *I **was** taller* becomes quite another proposition when we insert one little word: *If I **were** taller.*

Why is this? It's because there's a special, "what if" sort of grammar that kicks in when we talk about something that's untrue. When we're in this iffy mood (the subjunctive mood, if you want to be technical), *was* becomes *were*. This happens when a sentence or a clause (a group of words with its own subject and verb) starts with *if,* and what's being talked about is contrary to fact:

*If I **were** king, no one would pay retail.* (I'm not king.)

*If she **were** older, she'd know better.* (She's not older.)

*We could go shopping if it **were** Saturday.* (Today is not Saturday.)

> **NOTE:** Not all *if* statements fall into this category, only those that are undeniably contrary to fact. In cases where the statement may actually be true, *was* remains *was*.
>
> *If I **was** rude, I apologize.* (I may have been rude.)
>
> *If she **was** there, I guess I missed her.* (She may have been there.)
>
> *If it **was** Thursday, I must have gone to bed early.* (It may have been Thursday.)

As If You Didn't Know

The same rules that apply to *if* statements apply to those starting with *as if* or *as though*:

*He acts as if he **were** infallible.*

(He's not infallible.)

*She behaves as though money **were** scarce.*

(Money is not scarce.)

Suggestive Language

Sometimes, English slips through a time warp and into another dimension. In cases where we'd normally use the verbs *was* or *were,* we use *be* instead. You might have wondered why, for example, we say, *I was quiet,* but *They requested that I be quiet.* What's going on here? The answer is that in English we have a special way of suggesting or demanding something (here's another example of the subjunctive mood). This is what you need to remember:

Use *be* instead of *was* or *were* after someone *suggests, demands, asks, requests, requires,* or *insists* that something be done:

I demanded that I be excused.

The judge ordered that he be executed.

Olivia insists they be admitted free.

The law requires that you be fingerprinted.

If *be* sounds unnatural to your ear, just imagine an unspoken *should* in front of it:

I demanded that I (should) be excused.

The judge ordered that he (should) be executed.

Olivia insisted they (should) be admitted free.

The law requires that you (should) be fingerprinted.

By the way, the form of the verb used here—*be* instead of *was* or *were*—is similar to the one used for a command: *Be good! Be quiet! Be there or be square!*

NOTE: Although *was, were,* and *be* give us the most trouble when we're suggesting or demanding something, other verbs must also be in the command form when they're forced to give "command" performances: *Mom demands that Ricky **eat**. We insist that she **walk**. He urged that Barbra **negotiate**. I suggested he **go**.* Again, if this feels unnatural, imagine an unspoken *should* in front of the verb: *I suggested he (should) **go**.*

Mayday! Mayday!

If there were a club for people who confuse *may* and *might,* I would be its president. Also its vice-president, treasurer, and recording secretary. I'm always using the search function on my computer to find *may* in my work, because it is often wrong and should be *might*.

May is a source of our word *maybe,* and that's a good clue to how it's used. We attach it to another verb (*happen,* for example) to indicate the possibility of something's happening. If we say something *may* happen, we mean it's possible or even probable.

Might is a slightly weaker form of *may.* Something that *might* happen is a longer shot than something that *may* happen. *I **may** get a raise* is more promising than *I **might** get a raise*.

Although your dictionary will tell you that *might* is the past tense of *may*, either one can be used in the present tense (*She **may** break a leg; She **might** break a leg*) or in the past (*She **may** have broken a leg; She **might** have broken a leg*). The form you choose depends on the degree of possibility.

There's an exception to this "possibility" rule, which is why I'm grateful for search keys. If a sentence has other verbs in the past tense, use only *might*: *She thought* [past] *she **might** have broken a leg. Eloise was* [past] *afraid they **might** lose everything. Frank said* [past] *he **might** leave early.*

By the way, don't mix up the *may* of possibility with the other *may*, the one that gives permission; see *can/may,* page 93.

Just One of Those Things

Here's one of the things that [*drives* or *drive*] us crazy. Should the verb be singular or plural? *Drives?* Or *drive?* In other words, what kind of verb goes with a phrase like *one of the, one of those,* or *one of these?* The answer in a nutshell:

- If *that* or *who* comes before the verb, it's plural: *He's one of the authors who **say** it best.*
- If not, it's singular: *One of the authors **says** it best.*

In the first example, *one* is not the subject of the verb *say.* The actual subject is *who,* which is plural because it refers to *authors.* In the second example, the subject really is *one.* If you don't trust me, just turn the sentences around in your mind and you'll end up with the correct verbs: *Of the authors who **say** it best, he is one. Of the authors, one **says** it best.*

Never-Never Land

Poor verbs! We tend to spread them a little thin sometimes. Any sentence with *never have and never will* is doomed. There's no way to finish it correctly, because there's almost no verb that goes with both *have* and *will.*

Here's the kind of sentence I mean: *They **never have and never will** forget Paris.* What we intend to say is, *They never have forgotten and never will forget Paris.* But what we've actually said is, *They never have [forget] and never will forget Paris.* That odd, crackling noise you hear is the sound of a sentence short-circuiting! This problem comes up whenever we use *have* and *will* with the same verb. Another major culprit is *always have and always will.*

Only when a verb appears the same way twice (like *forget* in *I never could forget and never would forget Paris*) can you omit the first one and avoid repeating yourself: *I never could and never would forget Paris.*

NOTE: If you don't want to repeat yourself when using different forms of the same verb, you can cheat by rearranging the sentence: *They never have forgotten Paris and never will*. That way, the part you're omitting—*forget Paris*—is at the end of the sentence, where it won't be missed very much. This isn't perfect grammar, mind you, but it's reasonable. And nobody will blow a fuse.

Ize in Our Heads: Are These Verbs Legit?

For centuries, we've been creating instant verbs in English simply by adding *ize* to nouns (*demon* ⇒ *demonize,* for instance) or to adjectives (*brutal* ⇒ *brutalize*). The ancient Greeks were the ones who gave us the idea. The *ize* ending (often *ise* in British spellings) has given us loads of useful words (*agonize, burglarize, fantasize, mesmerize, pasteurize, pulverize*). It's just as legitimate to add *ize* to the end of a word as it is to add *un* or *pre* to the beginning.

Yet there can be too much of a good thing, and that's what has happened with *ize*. Verbs should be lively little devils, and just adding *ize* to a word doesn't give it life. Fortunately, many recent horrors (*credibilize, permanentize, respectabilize, uniformize*) didn't catch on. But some lifeless specimens have slipped into the language, among them *colorize, prioritize,* and *finalize,* and they're probably going to be around for a while.

Infinitively Speaking

Many of us misuse the infinitive (a verb that usually has *to* in front of it) after certain words. *Anxious*, for example. Are you *anxious to go*, or are you *anxious about going*? If you picked *anxious to go*, you should be anxious about your grammar. Here's a list of words that shouldn't be followed by infinitives:

anxious: *I was* **anxious about going**. Not: *I was anxious to go*. With the infinitive, use *eager* instead: *I was* **eager to go**.

convince: *They* **convinced** *us* **that** *we should go*. Not: *They convinced us to go*. With the infinitive, use *persuade*: *They* **persuaded** *us* **to** *go*. For more about *convince* and *persuade*, see page 95.

prevent: *We* **prevented** *him* **from** *going*. Not: *We prevented him to go*. If you keep the infinitive, use *did not permit* instead: *We* **did not permit** *him* **to** *go*. Another way to say this is: *We* **prevented** *his going*.

prohibit: *She was* **prohibited from** *going*. Not: *She was prohibited to go*. With the infinitive, use *forbid*: *She was* **forbidden to** *go*. For more about *forbid* and *prohibit*, see pages 110 and 112.

I have two pieces of advice about verbs ending in *ize*:

- Don't coin any new ones.
- Don't use any recent ones you don't like. If we ignore them, maybe they'll go away.

Ants at the Picnic: Pesky Look-alikes

Who hasn't confused *lie* and *lay*? *Sit, set,* and *sat*? *Rise* and *raise*? It's nothing to be ashamed of. You could commit them all to memory, of course. Or you could *lay* your cares aside, *sit* tight, *rise* to the occasion, and look up the answer.

Here's the *lay* of the land (or, as they say in Britain, the *lie* of the land):

Lie (to recline): *She **lies** quietly. Last night, she **lay** quietly. For years, she **has lain** quietly.*

Lie (to fib): *He **lies**. Yesterday he **lied**. Frequently he **has lied**.*

Lay (to place): *She **lays** it there. Yesterday she **laid** it there. Many times she **has laid** it there.* (When *lay* means "to place," it's always followed by an object, the thing being placed.)

Sit (to be seated): *I **sit**. I **sat** last week. I **have sat** many times.*

Set (to place): *He **sets** it there. He **set** it there yesterday. He **has set** it there frequently.* (*Set* meaning "to place" is always followed by an object, the thing being placed.)

Rise (to go up or get up): *You **rise**. You **rose** at seven. You **have risen** even earlier.*

Raise (to bring something up): *I **raise** it. I **raised** it last year. I **have raised** it several times.* (The verb *raise* is always followed by an object, the thing being brought up.)

Fitted to Be Tied

Several verbs ending in *t* or *d* have all but dropped the *ed* ending in the past tense. Once we would have said, *Mr. Cratchit **quitted** the firm, **betted** on the horses, and **wetted** his whistle, then **wedded** his sweetheart in a suit that **fitted** him perfectly.* The British still use those endings, but Americans are now more likely to use the shorter *quit, bet, wet, wed,* and *fit. Mr. Cratchit **quit** the firm, **bet** on the horses, and **wet** his whistle, then **wed** his sweetheart in a suit that **fit** him perfectly.*

We still use *wedded,* but only as an adjective (a word that describes people or things): ***Wedded** life is a thrill a minute.*

We also use *fitted* as an adjective (*a fitted sheet, a fitted suit*). And we use *fitted* when we speak of someone whose clothes are, shall we say, under construction: *Alice was **fitted** for a new dress.* But later we would say, *When it was finished, the dress **fit** like a glove.*

Happy Endings: Burned or Burnt?

He *spilled* the milk, or he *spilt* it? He *burned* the toast, or he *burnt* it? Actually, they're all correct, although in these cases the *ed* spellings are preferred.

A number of verbs can form the past tense with either *ed* or *t*. For some of them, the preferred ending is *ed,* and for others it's *t*. In these examples, the favored spellings are given first, and the less common ones follow in parentheses: *bereaved* (*bereft*), *dreamed* (*dreamt*), *dwelt* (*dwelled*), *knelt* (*kneeled*), *leaned* (*leant*), *leapt* (*leaped*), *learned* (*learnt*), *smelled* (*smelt*), *spelled* (*spelt*), *spoiled* (*spoilt*).

> **NOTE:** Some verbs that form the past tense by adding *t* have no alternative *ed* endings. The ones we see most often are *crept, dealt, felt, kept, left, lost, meant, slept, swept,* and *wept*.

Wake-up Calls

Wake . . . woke . . . have *woken*? Sorry, *woken* is no way to talk. Many dictionaries list *woken* as an alternative form, but it's considered obsolete.

The correct forms of the verb *wake* are *wake, woke,* and

have waked. Here they are in action: *I **wake** at seven. Yesterday I **woke** at seven. In the past, I **have waked** much later.* By the way, it's fine to add *up* to any of the *wake* forms: *wake up, woke up, have waked up.*

If you're like me, and you think *have waked* sounds weird, try *have wakened* or *have awakened*. Those are past tenses of related verbs, *waken* and *awaken*.

There are plenty of ways to greet the morning—maybe more than we need. You can *wake,* or you can *waken,* or you can *awake,* or you can *awaken.* So get up, already!

What's the Use?

One way to say *he formerly did* is *he used to: Andre **used to** have a good lob.*

What about when the sentence becomes a question or a negative statement? Let's see if we can choose the right form:

*Did Andre [**use** or **used**] to have a good lob?*

*Andre didn't [**use** or **used**] to have a good lob.*

The answer in both cases is *use*. Why? Because *did use* is another way of saying *used,* just as *did walk* is another way of saying *walked.* You wouldn't say "did walked," would you? Then why would you say "did used"?

NOTE: The British, as you might have noticed, have a different way of dealing with *used to*. Instead of using *did* in a question or a negative statement, they prefer these forms: *Used Andre to have a good lob? Andre usedn't to have a good lob.* Forget you ever saw them.

Getting the Hang of Hung

No! It's not true that *hung* is never right. I would like to impress this on the magazine writer who described somebody's walls as "hanged with handsome black-and-white photographs."

Both past tenses have been around for hundreds of years, but since the sixteenth century it's been customary to reserve *hanged* for referring to executions, and to use *hung* for other meanings.

So, except at the gallows, *hung* is the correct past tense of *hang*: *He **hung** around. They **have hung** around.* This is true whether you've *hung* pictures, *hung* loose, *hung* out, *hung* laundry, or *hung* up.

Anyone who still uses *hanged* in such cases should be suspended.

That's That

There are two kinds of editors. One kind sticks in *that* wherever it will fit. The other kind takes it out.

They're both wrong.

Many verbs (*think, say, hope, believe, find, feel,* and *wish* are examples) sound smoother—to my ears, at least—when they're followed by *that*: *He believed [**that**] Bob was embezzling.* You may agree that the sentence sounds better with *that,* or you may not. It's purely a matter of taste. The sentence is correct either way.

Some writers and editors believe that if *that* can logically follow a verb, it should be there. Others believe that if *that* can logically be omitted, it should be taken out. If you like it, use it. If you don't, don't. Here are some cases where adding *that* can rescue a drowning sentence.

- When a time element comes after the verb: *Bob said on Friday he would confess.* This could mean either: *Bob said **that** on Friday he would confess,* or *Bob said on Friday **that** he would confess.* So why not add a *that* and make yourself clear?
- When the point of the sentence comes late: *Frank found the old violin hidden in a trunk in his attic wasn't a real Stradivarius.* Better: *Frank found **that** the old violin hidden in a trunk in his attic wasn't a real Stradivarius.*

Otherwise, we have to read to the end of the sentence to learn that Frank's finding the violin isn't the point.

● When there are two more verbs after the main one: *Hilda thinks the idea stinks and Horace does too.* According to the sentence, what exactly is Hilda thinking? It could mean *Hilda thinks **that** the idea stinks and **that** Horace does too.* Or it could mean *Hilda thinks **that** the idea stinks, and Horace does too.* Adding *that* (and a well-placed comma) can make clear who's thinking what.

Splitsville

Many people seem to believe that there's something sacred about a verb, and that it's wrong to split up one that comes in parts (*had gone* or *would go,* for example). You've probably heard at one time or another that you're cheating if you slip a word (say, *finally*) in between (as in *had finally gone* or *would finally go*). Well, it just isn't so.

The best place to put a word like *finally*—that is, an adverb, a word that characterizes a verb—is directly before the action being described: in this case, *go* or *gone*. It's perfectly natural to split the parts of a verb like *have gone* by putting an adverb between them: *The cowboys **have finally gone**.* If you prefer to put the adverb before or after all the parts of the verb (as in, *The cowboys **finally have gone**,* or *The cowboys* *have gone finally*), that's all right, too. But don't go out of your way to avoid the "splits." And keep in mind that adverbs usually do the most good right in front of the action words they describe.

This fear of splitting verb phrases, by the way, has its origins in another old taboo—the dreaded "split infinitive" (*to finally go,* for instance). The chapter on dead rules has more on that one, and on how the myth got started. See page 182.

The Willies: Will or Shall?

In George Washington's day, schoolchildren on both sides of the Atlantic were admonished to use *shall* instead of *will* in some cases. (Don't ask!) Americans have since left *shall* behind and now use *will* almost exclusively. Although *shall* survives in parts of England, even the British are using it less and less these days.

Shall can still be found in a few nooks and crannies of American English, such as legalese (*This lease* **shall** *commence on January 1*) and lofty language (*We* **shall** *overcome*). It's also used with *I* and *we* in some kinds of questions—when we're asking what another person wishes: **Shall** *we dance, or* **shall** *I fill your glass?*

Shall is one of the "living dead" discussed in the chapter on outdated rules, page 188.

The Incredible Shrinking Words: Contractions

The contraction—two words combined into one, as in *don't* or *I'm*—seldom gets a fair shake from English teachers. It may be tolerated, but it's looked down upon as colloquial or, according to one expert, "dialect" (what a slur!). Yet despite its esteem problem, the humble contraction is used every day by virtually everyone, and has been for centuries. Quaint antiquities like *shan't* (shall not), *'tis* (it is), *'twas* (it was), *'twill* (it will), *'twould* (it would), and even *'twon't* (it will not) are evidence of the contraction's long history.

Today's contractions always include a verb; the other word is either a subject or the word "not."

Isn't it time we admitted that the contraction has earned its place in the sun? It has all the qualities we admire in language: it's handy, succinct, and economical, and everybody knows what it means. Contractions are obviously here to stay, so why not give them a little respect? Here's the long and the short of it: the contractions that are respectable, followed by a few that aren't.

FIT TO PRINT

aren't	are not	must not	mustn't
can't	cannot	ought not	oughtn't
couldn't	could not	she'd	she would;
didn't	did not		she had
doesn't	does not		(*not*
don't	do not		she did)
hadn't	had not	she'll	she will
hasn't	has not	she's	she is;
haven't	have not		she has
he'd	he would;	shouldn't	should not
	he had	that's	that is;
	(*not* he did)		that has
he'll	he will	there's	there is;
he's	he is;		there has
	he has	they'd	they would;
I'd	I would;		they had
	I had		(*not*
	(*not* I did)		they did)
I'll	I will	they'll	they will
I'm	I am	they're	they are
I've	I have	they've	they have
isn't	is not	wasn't	was not
it'll	it will	we'd	we would;
it's	it is; it has		we had
let's	let us		(*not* we did)
mightn't	might not	we'll	we will

we're	we are	who're	who are
we've	we have	who's	who is;
weren't	were not		who has
what'll	what will	who've	who have
what're	what are	won't	will not
what's	what is;	wouldn't	would not
	what has	you'd	you would;
what've	what have		you had
who'd	who would;		(*not*
	who had		you did)
	(*not*	you'll	you will
	who did)	you're	you are
who'll	who will	you've	you have

OUT OF BOUNDS

ain't. It's not OK and it never will be OK. Get used to it. If you're tempted to use it to show that you have the common touch, make clear that you know better: *Now, **ain't** that a shame!*

could've, should've, would've, might've, must've. There's a good reason to stay away from writing these. Seen in print, they encourage mispronunciation, which explains why they're often heard as *could of, should of, would of, might of,* and *must of* (or, even worse, *coulda, shoulda, woulda, mighta,* and *musta*). It's fine to pronounce these as though the *h* in *have* were silent. But let's not forget that *have* is there. Write it out.

it'd, that'd, there'd, this'd, what'd. Notice how these 'd endings seem to add a syllable that lands with a *thud?* And they look ridiculously clumsy in writing. Let's use the 'd contractions (for *had* or *would*) only with *I, you, he, she, we, they,* and *who.*

that'll, that're, that've, there'll, there're, there've, this'll. Ugh! These clumsies may be fine in conversation, but written English isn't ready for them yet. Do I use *that'll* when I talk? Sure. But not when I write.

when'll, when're, when's, where'd, where'll, where're, where's, why're, why's, why've. Resist the urge to write any contractions with *why, when,* or *where.* We all say things like, "*Where's Raoul, and why's he late?"* But don't put them in writing, Waldo or no Waldo.

gonna, gotta, wanna. These are merely substandard English. Unless you're talking to your sister on the phone, make it *going to, got to, want to,* and so on.

Where There's a Will, There's a Would

Do you waffle when faced with the choice of *will* or *would?* Take your pick: *Harry said he [will or would] make waffles for breakfast.*

All Tensed Up

If we used only one verb per sentence, we'd never have trouble choosing the tense—past, present, future, or whatever: *They waltzed. He tangos. She will polka.* And so on. Many sentences, though, have several things going on in them— actions happening at different times, each with its own verb. You can't just string these verbs together like beads in a necklace. It takes planning.

With most sentences, we don't give this much thought, and we don't have to. When all the actions happen at about the same time, we can just put them in the same tense and rattle them off in order: *On Sundays, Elaine **rises** at seven, **makes** tea, **showers**, and **goes** back to bed. Last Sunday, Elaine **rose** at seven, **made** tea, **showered**, and **went** back to bed.*

When we have different things happening at distinctly different times, sentences get more complicated: *Elaine **says** she **made** tea last Sunday, but she **will make** coffee next week.*

Common sense tells us how to do most of these adjustments in timing. But some verb sequences are harder to sort out than others. Pages 77–80 deal with some of the most troublesome ones.

Follow the lead of the first verb (*said*). Since it's in the past tense, use *would*: *Harry said he* **would** *make waffles for breakfast*. When the first verb is in the present tense (*says*), use *will*: *Harry says he* **will** *make waffles for breakfast*.

Now here's an example with three verbs (the same principle applies): *Harry thought that if he [eats or* **ate***] one waffle, he [***will** *or* **would***] want another*.

Since the first verb (*thought*) is in the past, use the past tense, *ate*, and *would*: *Harry thought that if he* **ate** *one waffle, he* **would** *want another*. When the first verb is in the present (*thinks*), use the present tense, *eats*, and *will*: *Harry thinks that if he* **eats** *one waffle, he* **will** *want another*.

In the Land of If

Think of *if* as a tiny set of scales. When a sentence has *if* in it, the verbs have to be in balance. When the *if* side of the scale is in the present tense, the other side calls for *will*. When the *if* side of the scale is in the past tense, the other side gets a *would*.

If he **shops** [present] *alone, he* **will spend** *too much*.

If he **shopped** [past] *alone, he* **would spend** *too much*.

Balancing the scales becomes more complicated as the tenses get more complicated. When you use a compound tense with *has* or *have* on the *if* side of the scale, you need a *will have* on the other side. Similarly, when you use a compound tense with *had* on the *if* side of the scale, you need a *would have* on the other.

If he **has shopped** alone, he **will have spent** too much.

If he **had shopped** alone, he **would have spent** too much.

The *if* part doesn't have to come first, but the scales must stay in balance: *He **will spend** too much if he **shops** alone. He **would spend** too much if he **shopped** alone.*

After Thoughts

Some people tense up when one action comes after another in a sentence. Let's test your tension level. Which verbs would you pick in these examples?

*I will start dinner after the guests [**arrive** or **have arrived**].*

*I started dinner after the guests [**arrived** or **had arrived**].*

If you chose the simpler ones, you were right: *I will start dinner after the guests **arrive**. I started dinner after the guests **arrived**.* Why make things harder than they have to be?

No matter what the tense of the main part of a sentence, and no matter how complicated, the verb that follows *after* should be in either the simple present (*arrive*) or the simple past (*arrived*).

When the main action in a sentence takes place in the present or in a future tense, the verb that follows *after* is in the simple present:

*I start dinner after the guests **arrive**. I will have started dinner after the guests **arrive**.*

When the main action takes place in a past tense, the verb that follows *after* is in the simple past:

*I would have started dinner after the guests **arrived**.*

The rule is the same if the sentence is turned around so the *after* part comes first: *After the guests **arrive**, I will have started dinner.*

Sometimes the simple solution is the best. Keep that in mind, and may all your verbs live happily ever after.

To Have or Not to Have

Have is a useful word, but we can have too much of it.

Which is correct? *I would have liked **to go**,* or *I would have liked **to have gone**.*

The first example is correct. One *have* is enough, though it can go with either half of the sentence: *I would **have** liked to go,* or *I would like to **have** gone.*

Here's a case in which even one *have* is a *have* too many.

Incorrect: *Two years ago, Whiskers was the first cat to have flown on the Concorde.*

Correct: *Two years ago, Whiskers was the first cat to fly on the Concorde.*

You need to use *have* only if you're talking about two different times in the past: *Until last year, Whiskers was the only cat* **to have flown** *on the Concorde.* If you find the concept hard to grasp, think of it this way. One of the times was last year and the other was the period before that: *Until last year, Whiskers was [at that time] the only cat* **to have flown** *[prior to that] on the Concorde.*

I could go on about the subtleties of *have,* but I suspect that by now you've had it.

Chapter 5

Verbal Abuse

Words on the Endangered List

The give-and-take of language is something like warfare. A word bravely soldiers on for years, until one day it falls face-down in the trenches, its original meaning a casualty of misuse. *Unique* is a good example: a crisp and accurate word meaning "one of a kind," now frequently degraded to merely "unusual."

Then there are what I call mixed doubles: pairs of words and phrases that are routinely confused, like *affect* and *effect*. Finally, there are the words that are mispronounced, misspelled, or so stretched out of shape that they aren't even words anymore—like that impostor *irregardless*. Keep in mind, though, that today's clumsy grotesquerie may be tomorrow's bon mot. The phrase *live audience* was a silly redundancy before sound and video recording came along.

Speaking of technology, a computer spelling checker is a

81

wonderful resource—I don't know what I'd do without mine—but don't depend too much on it. For instance, my spell-check software tells me that *restauranteur* and *judgement* and *straightlaced* are spelled correctly, but I know better. And it doesn't care how I use *affect* and *effect,* as long as they're spelled right.

Here are some of the most commonly mauled words and phrases, and tips on how to rescue them. Bloodied but unbowed, an abused word shouldn't be given up for dead. Give it back its proper meaning, spelling, usage, and pronunciation, and it will live to fight another day.

What's the Meaning of This?

decimate. Who says grammar books don't have sex and violence? To *decimate* means literally "to slaughter every tenth one," although most people don't intend it literally. It can be used loosely to mean "to destroy in part" (*Gomez says the mushroom crop in the cellar has been **decimated** by rats*), but don't use it to mean "to destroy entirely." And definitely don't attach a figure to the damage: *The earthquake **decimated** seventy-five percent of Morticia's antiques.* Ouch!

diagnose. The disease is *diagnosed,* not the patient. *Miss Mapp's rash was **diagnosed** as shingles.* Not: *Miss Mapp was **diagnosed** with shingles.*

dilemma. This is no ordinary problem; the *di* (from the Greek for "twice") is a clue that there's a *two*ness here. A *dilemma* is a situation involving two choices—both of them bad. (This idea is captured neatly in the old phrase about being caught on the *horns of a dilemma*.) *Richie faced a dilemma: he could wear the green checked suit with the gravy stain, or the blue one with the hole.*

eclectic. This word is mistakenly used to mean discriminating or sophisticated; in fact, it means "drawn from many sources." *Sherman has an eclectic assortment of mud-wrestling memorabilia.*

effete. Don't use this if you mean weak, effeminate, soft, or affected. *Effete* means barren, used up, or worn out. *Frazier considers abstract expressionism an effete art form.*

enervating. Energizing it's not. On the contrary: if something's *enervating*, it drains you of energy. *Frazier's date found his conversation enervating.*

enormity. Don't confuse this with *enormousness,* because *enormity* isn't a measure of size alone. It refers to something immensely wicked, monstrous, or outrageous. *Sleepy little Liechtenstein was shocked by the enormity of the crime.*

fortuitous. No, this word doesn't mean fortunate or lucky. *Fortuitous* means accidental or by chance. *It was entirely fortuitous that Potsie washed his car just before it rained.*

fulsome. You may think this means abundant or flattering. Actually, it means overdone or disgustingly excessive. *Ed-*

*die's insincere and **fulsome** speeches got on Mrs. Cleaver's nerves.*

hero. There was a time when this word was reserved for people who were . . . well . . . heroic. People who performed great acts of bravery or valor, often facing danger, even death. But lately, *hero* has started losing its luster. We hear it applied indiscriminately to professional athletes, lottery winners, and kids who clean up at spelling bees. There's no other word quite like *hero,* so let's not bestow it too freely. It would be a pity to lose it. *Achilles was a **hero**.*

hopefully. By now it's probably hopeless to resist the misuse of *hopefully.* Strictly speaking, there's only one way to use it correctly—as an adverb meaning "in a hopeful manner." (*"I'm thinking of going to Spain,"* said Eddie. *"Soon?"* Mrs. Cleaver asked **hopefully**.) In an ideal world, it wouldn't be used to replace a phrase like "It is hoped" or "I hope," as in: *"**Hopefully** the cuisine in Spain will be as delectable as your own,"* Eddie said. But of course it *is* used that way. In the time it takes you to read this sentence, *hopefully* will be misused at least once by every man, woman, and child in the United States. (Well, that may be a bit of hyperbole; see page 114.) Whether we like it or not—and I don't—*hopefully* seems to be joining that class of introductory words (*happily, sadly, honestly, frankly, seriously,* and others) that we use not to describe a verb, which is what adverbs usually do, but to describe our own attitude toward the statement that follows. When I say, "Sadly, somebody else won the jackpot," I don't mean the other guy was sad about winning. I mean, "I'm sad to say that somebody else won the jackpot." And "Frankly, he disgusts me" doesn't mean the poor guy is disgusting in a frank way. It means, "I'm frank when I say that he disgusts me." So there you have it. Join the crowd and abuse *hopefully* if you want; I can't stop you. But maybe if enough of us preserve the original meaning it can be saved. One can only hope.

irony. I hope some TV news reporters are tuning in. A wonderful word for a wonderful idea, *irony* refers to a sly form of expression in which you say one thing and mean another. (*"You're wearing the green checked suit again, Richie! How fashionable of you," said Mrs. Cunningham, her voice full of irony*.) A situation is *ironic* if the result is the opposite—or pretty much so—of what was intended. It isn't merely coincidental or surprising, as when the newscaster thoughtlessly reports, "Ironically, the jewelry store was burglarized on the same date last year." If the burglars take great pains to steal what turns out to contain a homing device that leads the police to them, that's *ironic*. (And forget the correct but clunky *ironical*.)

literally. This means actually or to the letter. (*Martha Stewart sprayed a dried bouquet with metallic paint, **literally** gilding the lily*.) *Literally* is often confused with *figuratively*, which means metaphorically or imaginatively. No one says *figuratively*, of course, because it doesn't have enough oomph. I am reminded of a news story, early in my editing career in Iowa, about a Pioneer Days celebration, complete with covered wagons and costumed "settlers." Our reporter proposed to say that spectators "were literally turned inside out and shot backwards in time." Gee, we should have sent a photographer along. (For the proper use of *backward,* see **toward**, page 116.)

livid. This isn't the colorful adjective you may think it is. *Livid* doesn't mean red or flushed (as in vivid or florid)—at least not yet. It means bluish, black-and-blue, or ashen. (*"The corpse is **livid**, Inspector," said Dr. Watson. "Obviously he's been dead for some time."*) Stay tuned, however. Dictionaries have started to notice that *livid* is sometimes taken to mean red, so change may be on the way.

noisome. If you think this means noisy, you're not even close. *Noisome* and *noisy* are as different as your nose and your ear. *Noisome* means evil-smelling or offensive. It's related to *annoy,* so think of it as a clipped form of *annoysome. The **noisome** fumes of the stink bomb forced officials to evacuate the school.*

presently. Misuse strikes again. If Kramer tells his landlord he's *presently* sending his rent, does that mean . . . uh . . . the check is in the mail, or the check really *is* in the mail? The answer is, don't hold your breath. *Presently* doesn't mean now or at present. It means soon, before long, any minute (hour, day) now, forthwith, shortly, keep your shirt on, faster than you can say Jack Robinson, or when I'm darn good and ready.

restive. Here's one that's worse than it sounds. *Restive* doesn't mean impatient or fidgety (that's *restless*). It means unruly or stubborn. *Even on a good day, Pugsley is a restive child.*

scarify. Sounds terrifying, doesn't it? Well, it's not. *Scarify* doesn't mean scare. Primarily, it means cut or scratch marks into the surface of something. A memory hint: If you *scarify* something, you leave *scars*. *Ricky promised that his Rollerblades wouldn't scarify the floor.*

unique. If it's *unique*, it's the one and only. It's unparalleled, without equal, incomparable, nonpareil, unrivaled, one of a kind. In other words, there's nothing like it—anywhere. There are no degrees of uniqueness, because the unique is absolute. Nothing can be more, less, sort of, rather, quite, very, slightly, or particularly *unique*. The word stands alone, like *dead, unanimous,* and *pregnant. The Great Wall of China is unique.*

via. This means "by way of," not "by means of." *Seiji drove to Tanglewood via Boston.* Not: *Seiji drove to Tanglewood via car.*

Mixed Doubles

abjure/adjure. The first means swear off. The second means command. *"Abjure cigars or move out of the house!" Ethel adjured Fred.*

abridge/bridge. To *abridge* something is to shorten it (think of the word *abbreviate*). An *abridged* book, for instance, is a condensed version. To *bridge* something means what you'd expect—to connect or to span a gap. *The producers hope to **abridge** Philip's nine-hour opera about an engineer who tries to **bridge** the Grand Canyon.*

accept/except. To *accept* something is to take it or agree to it. *Except* can also be a verb—it means exclude or leave out—but its usual meaning is "other than." *"I never **accept** presents from men," said Lorelei, "**except** when we've been properly introduced."*

adverse/averse. The longer word is the stronger word. *Adverse* implies hostility or opposition, and usually characterizes a thing or an action. *Averse* implies reluctance or unwillingness, and usually characterizes a person. *Georgie was not **averse** to inoculation, until he had an **adverse** reaction to the vaccine.*

affect/effect. If you're referring to a thing (a noun), ninety-nine times out of a hundred you mean *effect*. (*The termites had a startling **effect** on the piano.*) If you mean an action (a verb), the odds are just as good if you go for *affect*. (*The problem **affected** Lucia's recital.*)

> **NOTE:** Then there's that one time out of a hundred. Here are the less common meanings for each of these words:
>
> • *Affect,* when used as a noun (pronounced with the accent on the first syllable), is a psychological term for "feeling." *Termites display a lack of **affect**.*

- *Effect,* when used as a verb, means achieve or bring about. *An exterminator **effected** the removal of the termites.*

aggravate/irritate. They're not interchangeable. *Irritate* means inflame; *aggravate* means worsen. *Poison ivy **irritates** the skin. Scratching **aggravates** the itch.*

   Aggravate is widely used to mean vex or annoy. I find this irritating.

ago/since. Use one or the other, not both. *Fluffy died three days **ago***. Or: *It's been three days **since** Fluffy died.* Not: *It's been three days **ago since** Fluffy died.*

allude/refer. To *allude* is to mention indirectly or to hint at—to speak of something in a covert or roundabout way. (*Cyril suspected that the discussion of bad taste **alluded** to his loud pants.*) To *refer* is to mention directly. (*"They're plaid!" said Gussie, **referring** to Cyril's trousers.*)

allusion/illusion/delusion. An *allusion* is an indirect mention. (*Gussie's comment about burlesque was a snide **allusion** to Cyril's hand-painted tie.*) An *illusion* is a false impression. (*It created the **illusion** of a naked woman.*) A *delusion* is a deception. (*Cyril clung to the **delusion** that his tie was witty.*) *Delusion* is much stronger than *illusion,* and implies that Cyril has been misled or deceived—in this case, by himself.

alternate/alternative. The first means one after the other; the second means one instead of the other. *Walking* *requires* **alternate** *use of the left foot and the right. The* **alternative** *is to take a taxi.*

amid/among/between. Use *between* when referring to two. (*There was a heated exchange* **between** *Miss Bennet and Mr. Darcy.*) Use *among* when referring to three or more individuals. (*She said he had behaved superciliously* **among** *her friends.*) Use *amid* when the reference is to a quantity of something you don't think of as individual items. (*As Darcy stalked off, she lost sight of him* **amid** *the shrubbery.*)

anxious/eager. In ordinary speech, these are used interchangeably. But in writing, use *eager* unless there is actually an element of *anxiety* involved. And note that *eager* is followed by *to,* but *anxious* is followed by *about* or *for. Nancy is* **eager** *to have a pony, but Aunt Fritzi is* **anxious** *about the expense.*

appraise/apprise. *Appraise* means evaluate or size up; *apprise* means inform. *Sotheby's* **apprised** *Donald of the fact that his "Rembrandt" was* **appraised** *as worthless.*

as if/as though. These mean the same thing and can be used interchangeably. Once upon a time, *if* was one of the meanings of *though.* It's not anymore, except in the phrase *as though. Cliff and Norm looked* **as though** *they could use a drink.*

assume/presume. They're not identical. *Assume* is closer to suppose, or "take for granted"; the much stronger *presume* is closer to believe, dare, or "take too much for granted." *I can only* **assume** *you are joking when you* **presume** *to call yourself a plumber!*

N O T E : *Presume in the sense of believe gives us the adjective presumptive. And presume in the sense of "take too much for granted" gives us the adjective presumptuous. As her favorite nephew, Bertie was Aunt Agatha's* **presumptive** *heir. Still, it was* **presumptuous** *of him to measure her windows for new curtains.*

avert/avoid. *Avert* means prevent, ward off, or turn away. *Avoid* means shun or stay clear of. *Mr. Smithers* **avoided** *the open manhole,* **averting** *a nasty fall.*

bad/badly. When it's an activity being described, use *badly,* the adverb (a word that describes a verb; many adverbs, you'll notice, end in *ly*). When it's a condition or a passive state being described, use *bad,* the adjective (a word that describes a noun). *Ollie ran the race* **badly***; afterward, he looked* **bad** *and he smelled* **bad***.* If the difference still eludes you, try mentally substituting a pair of words less likely to be confused: *Ollie ran the race* **honestly***; afterward, he looked* **honest** *and he smelled* **honest***.*

The same logic applies for *well* and *good.* When it's an activity being described, use *well,* the adverb. (As you can see, not all adverbs end in *ly*.) When it's a condition or a passive state being described, use *good,* the adjective. *Stan sang* **well***; at the recital he looked* **good** *and he sounded* **good***.*

NOTE: There's a complication with *well*. It's a two-faced word that can be an adjective as well as an adverb. As an adjective, it means healthy (*Ollie feels well*).

beside/besides. *Beside* means "by the side of." *Besides* means "in addition" or "moreover." *Pip was seated **beside** Miss Havisham in an uncomfortable chair. He had a fly in his soup **besides**.*

bi/semi. In theory, *bi* attached to the front of a word means two and *semi* means half. (*Although Moose is bilingual, he's **semiliterate***.) In practice, *bi* sometimes means *semi,* and *semi* sometimes means *bi*. You're better off avoiding them when you want to indicate time periods; instead, use "every two years" or "twice a week" or whatever. I don't recommend using the following terms, but in case you run across them, here's what they mean. (You can see why they're confusing.)

biennial: every two years
biannual: twice a year *or* every two years (Here again, dictionaries tend to disagree, so they aren't much help.)
semiannual: every half-year
bimonthly: every two months *or* twice a month
semimonthly: every half-month
biweekly: every two weeks *or* twice a week
semiweekly: every half-week

both/as well as. Use one or the other, but not (ahem!) both. *Trixie had **both** a facial and a massage.* Or: *Trixie had a facial **as well as** a massage.*

bring/take. Which way is the merchandise moving? Is it coming or going? If it's coming here, someone's *bringing* it. If it's going there, someone's *taking* it. (*"**Bring** me my slippers,"* said Rhoda, *"and **take** away these stiletto heels!"*) That much is pretty straightforward, but there are gray areas where the *bringing* and the *taking* aren't so clear. Say you're a dinner guest and you decide to tote a bottle of wine along with you. Do you *bring* it or do you *take* it? The answer depends on your perspective—on which end of the journey you're talking about, the origin or the destination. "What shall I bring, white or red?" you ask the host. "Bring red," he replies. (Both you and he are speaking of the wine from the point of view of its destination—the host.) Ten minutes later, you're asking the wine merchant, "What should I take, a Burgundy or a Bordeaux?" "Take this one," she says. (Both you and she are speaking of the wine from the point of view of its origin.) Clear? If not, pour yourself a glass, take it easy, and say what sounds most natural. You'll probably be right.

callous/callus. One's an adjective (it characterizes something), and one's a noun. *Hard-hearted Hannah is **callous**, but the thing on her toe is a **callus**.*

can/may. The difference is between being able and being allowed or permitted. *Can* means able to; *may* means permitted to. *"I **can** fly when lift plus thrust is greater* *than load plus drag," said Sister Bertrille. "**May** I demonstrate?"*

NOTE: *May* is used in another sense: to indicate possibility. See the section on *may* and *might,* page 104.

chord/cord. A *chord* is a combination of musical notes; it has an *h,* for "harmony," which is what *chords* can produce. (*"That **chord** is a diminished seventh," said Ludwig.*) A *cord* is a string or cable, like the ones found in the human anatomy: spinal cord, umbilical cord, and vocal cords. (*Wolfgang never had to worry about tripping over an electrical **cord**.*) A mislaid rope may be called a *lost cord,* but the familiar musical phrase is *lost chord.*

compare with/compare to. Don't lose sleep over this one. The difference is subtle. *Compare with,* the more common phrase, means "to examine for similarities and differences." The less common *compare to* is used to show a resemblance: ***Compared with** Oscar, Felix is a crybaby. He once **compared** his trials **to** those of Job.*

complement/compliment. To *complement* is to complete, to round out, or to bring to perfection; a *complement* is something that completes or makes whole. (A little memory aid: Both *complement* and *complete* contain two *e*'s.) To *compliment* is to praise or admire; a *compliment* is an expression of praise or admiration. *Marcel loved to **compliment** Albertine. "That chemise **complements** your eyes, my little sparrow," he murmured.*

continually/continuously. Yes, there is a slight difference, although most people (and even many dictionaries) treat them the same. *Continually* means repeatedly, with breaks in between. *Continuously* means without interruption, in an unbroken stream. *Heidi has to wind the cuckoo clock **continually** to keep it running **continuously**.* (If it's important to emphasize the distinction, it's probably better to use *periodically* or *intermittently* instead of *continually* to describe something that starts and stops.) The same distinction, by the way, applies to *continual* and *continuous,* the adjective forms.

convince/persuade. You *convince* her *of* something. You *persuade* her *to do* something. *Convince* is usually followed by *of* or *that,* and *persuade* is followed by *to. **Father convinced** Bud **that** work would do him good, and **persuaded** him **to** get a job.* For more on *convince* and *persuade,* see page 63.

credibility/credulity. If you've got *credibility,* you're believable; you can be trusted. *Credulity* is a different quality—it means you'll believe whatever you're told; you're too trusting. The descriptive terms (adjectives) are *credible* (believable) and *credulous* (gullible). The opposites of these, respectively, are *incredible* (unbelievable) and *incredulous* (skeptical). *Councilman Windbag has lost his **credibility,** even among suckers known for their **credulity**.*

NOTE: Out in left field, meanwhile, is an entirely different player: *creditable,* which means deserving of credit, or praiseworthy.

deserts/desserts. People who get what they *deserve* are getting their *deserts*—the accent for both is on the second syllable. (*John Wilkes Booth got his just **deserts**.*) People who get goodies smothered in whipped cream and chocolate sauce at the end of a meal are getting *desserts*—which they may or may not deserve: *"For **dessert** I'll have one of those layered puff-pastry things with cream filling and icing on top," said Napoleon.*

differ from/differ with. In general, things *differ from* one another, but people who disagree *differ with* one another. (*Seymour insisted that his left foot **differed from** his right in size. His chiropodist, however, **differed with** him.*) In either sense, *differ* may be used alone: *Seymour says his feet differ. His chiropodist differs.*

different from/different than. What's the difference? The simple answer is that *different from* is almost always right, and *different than* is almost always wrong. You can stop there if you like.

NOTE: You may use either one just before a clause (a group of words with its own subject and verb). Both of these are accepted: *Respectability is **different from** what it was fifty years ago. Respectability is **different than** it was fifty years ago.*

discomfit/discomfort. Here's a horse that's gotten out of the barn. Back when men were men and words had some muscle, *discomfit* meant defeat, rout, or overthrow. A *discomfited* enemy may well have been a dead enemy. (*Robin Hood and his merry men **discomfited** the Sheriff of Nottingham.*) But *discomfit* seems to have lost its punch. Perhaps because of confusion with *discomfort* and *dismay,* it is often used to indicate uneasiness or vague dissatisfaction. Dictionaries have begun to accept this usage, a development I find *discomforting.*

discreet/discrete. If you're gossiping, you probably want *discreet,* a word that means careful or prudent. The other spelling, *discrete,* means separate, distinct, or unconnected. *Arthur was **discreet** about his bigamy. He managed to maintain two **discrete** households.*

disinterested/uninterested. They're not the same. *Disinterested* means impartial or neutral; *uninterested* means bored or lacking interest. *A good umpire should be **disinterested**, said Casey, but certainly not **uninterested**.*

each other/one another. The rule: Use *each other* for two, *one another* for three or more. (*Nick and Nora found **each other** adorable. Nick and his cousins all heartily despised **one another**.*) You'll never go wrong by following the rule, but keep in mind that many respected writers ignore it, using *one another* when referring to a pair. (*Husband and wife should respect **one another**.*) So if the more relaxed usage sounds better to your ear and you're not concerned about being strictly correct, allow yourself some latitude. (Speaking of *other* and *another,* here's a whole other issue. Some people combine *whole other* with *another* and end up with *a whole 'nother.* Ugh! Not that you or I would ever do such a thing, of course.)

e.g./i.e. Go ahead. Be pretentious in your writing and toss in an occasional *e.g.* or *i.e.* But don't mix them up. Clumsy inaccuracy can spoil that air of authority you're shooting for. *E.g.* is short for a Latin term, *exempli gratia,* that means "for example." (*Kirk and Spock had much in common,* **e.g.,** *their interest in astronomy and their concern for the ship and its crew.*) The more specific term *i.e.,* short for the Latin *id est,* means "that is." (*But they had one obvious difference,* **i.e.,** *their ears.*) Both *e.g.* and *i.e.* must have commas before and after (unless, of course, they're preceded by a dash or a parenthesis).

emigrate/immigrate. You *emigrate from* one country and *immigrate to* another. (*Grandma* **emigrated from** *Hungary in 1923, the same year that Grandpa* **immigrated to** *America.*) Whether you're called an *emigrant* or an *immigrant* depends on whether you're going or coming, and on the point of view of the speaker. A trick for remembering:

> *E*migrant as in *Exit.*
> *I*mmigrant as in *In.*

eminent/imminent/immanent. If you mean famous or superior, the word you want is *eminent.* If you mean impending or about to happen, the word is *immi-*

nent. If you mean inherent, present, or dwelling within, the word is the rarely heard *immanent. The **eminent** Archbishop Latour, knowing his death was **imminent**, felt God was **immanent**.*

> **NOTE:** The legal term is *eminent domain.*

farther/further. Use *farther* when referring to physical distance; use *further* to refer to abstract ideas or to indicate a greater extent or degree. *Lumpy insisted that he could walk no **farther**, and he refused to discuss it any **further**.*

faze/phase. To *faze* is to disconcert or embarrass; it comes from a Middle English word, *fesen,* which meant "drive away" or "put to flight." A *phase,* from the Greek word for "appear," is a stage or period of development; the word is used as a verb in the expressions *phase in* and *phase out,* to appear and disappear by stages. *Jean-Paul's infidelity is just a **phase**, says Simone, so she never lets it **faze** her.*

fewer/less. Use *fewer* to mean a smaller number of individual things; use *less* to mean a smaller quantity of something. *Mr. Flanders is a practical man. The **less** money he makes, the **fewer** dollars he spends.*

flounder/founder. To *flounder* is to stumble awkwardly or thrash about like a fish out of water. (*Harry **flounders** from one crisis to another.*) To *founder* is to get stuck, fail completely, or sink like a ship. (*His business **foundered** when the market collapsed.*)

flout/flaunt. *Flout* means defy or ignore. *Flaunt* means show off. *When Bruce ran that stop sign, he was **flouting** the law and **flaunting** his new Harley.*

gantlet/gauntlet. You run the *gantlet,* but you throw down the *gauntlet.* Why? It seems that in days of yore, a knight in a fighting mood would defiantly fling his *gauntlet* (a heavy, armored glove) to the ground as a challenge. To pick up the *gauntlet* was to accept the challenge. Meanwhile, a form of military punishment (a *gantlet,* from the Swedish word for the ordeal) required the hapless offender to run between parallel lines of his colleagues, who hit him with switches or clubs as he passed. It's a distinction worth preserving, even if some looser dictionaries no longer think so. *Wearing her mink to the ASPCA meeting, Zsa Zsa ran a **gantlet** of hostile stares. "So what?" she said, throwing down the **gauntlet**.*

good/well. These are cousins to **bad/badly** (page 91).

historic/historical. If something has a place in history, it's *historic.* If something has to do with the subject of history, it's *historical.* *There's not much **historical** evidence that the Hartletops' house is **historic**.*

hyper/hypo. Added to the front of a word, *hyper* means over or more; *hypo* means under or less. *I become **hyperactive** and get a rash if I don't use a **hypoallergenic** soap.*

if/whether. When you're talking about a choice between alternatives, use *whether*: *Richie didn't know **whether** he should wear the blue suit or the green one.* The giveaway is the presence of *or* between the alternatives. But if there's a *whether or not* choice (*Richie wondered **whether or not** he should wear his green checked suit*), you can usually drop the *or not* and use either *whether* or *if*: *Richie wondered **if** [or **whether**] he should wear his green checked suit.* Occasionally you'll need to keep *or not* for emphasis: *Richie wanted to wear the green one, **whether** it had a gravy stain **or not**.*

imply/infer. These words are poles apart. To *imply* is to suggest, or to throw out a suggestion; to *infer* is to conclude, or to take in a suggestion. *"You **imply** that I'm an idiot," said Stanley. "You **infer** correctly," said Blanche.*

in behalf of/on behalf of. The difference may be tiny, but it's worth knowing. *In behalf of* means "for the benefit of," or "in the interest of." *On behalf of* means "in place of," or "as the agent of." *Bertie presented the check **on behalf of** the Drones Club, to be used **in behalf of** the feebleminded.*

ingenious/ingenuous. Something that's *ingenious* (pronounced in-JEEN-yus) is clever or brilliant; the tip-off is that it has the pronunciation of *genius* built right in. *Ingenuous* (in-JEN-you-us) means frank, candid, innocently open; it's related to *ingénue,* a word for an inexperienced girl. (Calling someone *disingenuous*—insincere—is a roundabout way of saying he lies.)

in to/into. Yes, there is a difference! Don't combine *in* and *to* to form *into* just because they happen to land next to each other. *Into* is for entering something (like a room or a profession), for changing the form of something (an ugly duckling, for instance), or for making contact (with a friend or a wall, perhaps). *Get **into** the coach before it turns **into** a pumpkin, and don't bang **into** the door!* Otherwise, use *in to*. *Bring the guests **in to** me, then we'll all go **in to** dinner.* (You wouldn't go *into* dinner, unless of course you jumped *into* the soup tureen.) And be careful with *tune* and *turn: I think I'll **tune in to** my favorite TV show and **turn into** a couch potato.*

Still having a hard time with *into* and *in to*? Here's a trick to help keep them straight. If you can drop the *in* without losing the meaning, the term you want is *in to*. *Bring the guests [**in**] to me, then we'll all go [**in**] to dinner.* (Yes, there's also a difference between *on to* and *onto*, page 104.)

lay/lie. To *lay* is to place something; there's always a "something" that's being placed. To *lie* is to recline. *If you're not feeling well, **lay** your tools aside and **lie** down.* (These two get really confusing in the past tense. There's more about *lay* and *lie,* and how to use them in the past, on page 64.)

lend/loan. Only the strictest grammarians now insist that *loan* is the noun and *lend* is the verb, a distinction that is still adhered to in Britain (***Lend** me a pound, there's a good chap*). American usage allows that either *loan* or *lend* may be used as a verb (***Loan** me a few bucks till payday*). To my ears, though, *lend* and *lent* do sound a bit more polished than *loan* and *loaned*.

liable/likely. They're not interchangeable, but they come pretty close sometimes. Use *likely* if you mean probable or expected. Use *liable* if you mean bound by law or obligation (as in *liable for damages*), or exposed to risk or misfortune. *If Madeline goes skating, she's **liable** to fall, and not **likely** to try it again.*

like/as. Which of these is correct? *Homer tripped, [**as** or **like**] anyone would.* The answer is *as,* because it is followed by a clause, a group of words with both a subject (*anyone*) and a verb (*would*). If no verb follows, choose *like: Homer walks **like** a duck.*

Those are the rules, but the ground is shifting. In casual usage, *like* is gaining steadily on *as* (*She tells it **like** it is*), and on its cousins *as if* and *as though,* which are used to introduce clauses that are hypothetical or contrary to fact (*She eats chocolate **like** it's going out of style*).

The informal use of *like* to introduce a clause may be fine in conversation or casual writing, but for those occasions when you want to be grammatically correct, here's how to remember the "*as* comes before a clause" rule: Just think of the notorious old cigarette ad—"*Winston tastes good like a cigarette should*"—and do the opposite. On those more relaxed occasions, do as you like.

like/such as. Which is correct? *Veronica prefers cool colors, [**like** or **such as**] blue, violet, and aqua.* It's a matter of taste—either is acceptable. To my ear, *like* sounds better; *such as* has a more formal air. Of course, there are times when a bit of stiffness is appropriate: *"I've got my reasons for always using **like**," said Rufus T. Firefly. "**Such as?**" said Mrs. Teasdale.*

loath/loathe. The one without an *e* is an adjective describing somebody who's unwilling or reluctant, and it's usually followed by *to*: *Dmitri is **loath** to eat in Indian restaurants.* The one with an *e* is a verb: *He **loathes** chicken vindaloo.*

may/might. These are tricky. *Might* is sometimes used as the past tense of *may,* but not always. In the present, *might* is used rather than *may* to describe an iffier situation. Something that *might* happen is more of a long shot than something that *may* happen. For more, see page 59.

nauseated/nauseous. It's the difference between sick and sickening. You are made sick (*nauseated*) by something sickening (*nauseous*). Never say, *"I'm nauseous."* Even if it is true, it's not something you should admit. *"I'm **nauseated** by that **nauseous** cigar!"* said Ethel.

on to/onto. If you mean on top of or aware of, use *onto.* (*The responsibility shifted **onto** Milo's shoulders. "I'm really **onto** your shenanigans," he said.*) Otherwise, use *on to*: *Hang on to your hat.* Sometimes it helps to imagine a word like "ahead" or "along" between them: *Milo drove **on to** Chicago. He was moving **on to** better things.* (Confused about *in to* and *into*? See page 101.)

oral/verbal. They're not the same, though the meanings do overlap. *Oral* means by mouth or by spoken word. *Verbal* means by written or spoken word. That's why *verbal* is so easily misunderstood. What's a *verbal* contract? Written or spoken? It can be either. When it's important to make the distinction, use *oral* when you mean spoken, *written* when you mean written. In the words of Sam Goldwyn: "A verbal contract isn't worth the paper it's written on."

ought / ought to. Which is proper? You'll always be correct if you use *ought to.* Omit *to,* if you wish, in a negative statement: *Children **ought** not take candy from strangers. Pigs **ought** never be allowed in the kitchen.*

overwhelming / overweening. The more familiar *overwhelming* means just what you think it does—too much! *Overweening,* a useful word that we don't see very often, means conceited or pretentious. *The arrogance of that **overweening** little jerk is simply **overwhelming**.*

palate / palette / pallet. Maybe you don't have any trouble telling these apart, but I have to look them up every time. The *palate* is the roof of the mouth, and the word also refers to the sense of taste. A *palette,* the board a painter mixes colors on, is also a range of colors. A *pallet* is a rustic bed, usually a makeshift mattress of straw or some other humble material. *Vincent painted his supper, then ate it. Having satisfied his **palate**, he cleaned his **palette**, and retired to his **pallet**.*

presume / presumptive / presumptuous. See the discussion of **assume / presume**, page 90.

prophecy / prophesy. The *prophecy* (noun) is what's foretold. To *prophesy* (verb) is to foretell. As for pronunciation, *prophecy* ends in a "see," *prophesy* in a "sigh."

*Madame Olga charged $50 per **prophecy,** claiming she could **prophesy** fluctuations in the commodities market.*

rack/wrack. Are you *racked* with guilt, or *wracked*? Is tax time nerve-*racking,* or nerve-*wracking*? Are you on the brink of *rack* and ruin, or *wrack* and ruin? Most of the time, you are *racked* (tortured, strained, stretched, punished). Just think of the *rack,* the medieval instrument of torture. If you're *wracked,* on the other hand, you're destroyed—you're *wreckage* on the beach of life (the words *wrack* and *wreck* are related). In sum: *You are **racked** with guilt, you've had a nerve-**racking** time, and you're facing **wrack** and ruin.* Sounds as though you need a less stressful life!

raise/rise. To *raise* is to bring something up; there's always a "something" that's being lifted. To *rise* is to get up. *When they **raise** the flag, we all **rise**.* (There's more about *raise* and *rise,* and how they're used in the past tense, on page 65.)

ravage/ravish. When the ocean liner *Queen Elizabeth* caught fire and burned in Hong Kong harbor, a newspaper in Minnesota heralded the news with this headline: "Queen Elizabeth Ravished." What the headline writer meant was *ravaged,* meaning damaged or destroyed. There's an element of lust in *ravish,* which means to carry off (either by force or by emotion) or to rape. These days we're more likely to use *ravish* in the emotional than in the violent sense. *Though it was **ravaged** by the cleaners, the dress still looked **ravishing**.*

regretfully/regrettably. A person who's full of regret is *regretful,* and sighs *regretfully.* A thing that's a cause of regret is *regrettable,* and *regrettably* that's the situation. *Hazel* **regretfully** *swept up the Ming vase, which* **regrettably** *had smashed to smithereens.*

set/sit. To *set* is to place something; there's always a "something" that's being placed. To *sit* is to be seated. **Set** *the groceries on the counter and* **sit** *at the table.* (There's more about *set* and *sit,* and how they're used in the past tense, on page 64.)

spade/spayed. People who confuse these must drive veterinarians crazy. A *spade* is a small, skinny shovel. An altered female dog or cat is *spayed.* To *spade* a garden is to dig it up; to *spay* a cat is to keep her from having kittens. *Ashley took up a* **spade** *and* **spaded** *the flower bed, while Melanie took Boots to be* **spayed.**

stationary/stationery. If the *stationery* (paper) is *stationary* (fixed or still), you can write on it, and it won't move. (Hint: Both *stationery* and *paper* contain *er.*) *"If you haven't become* **stationary,** *Barney, please get up and bring me my* **stationery,**" *said Thelma Lou.*

than/then. Does it make your hair stand on end when someone writes: *"He's taller* **then** *his brother"*? No? Go stand in the corner. *Than* and *then* are similar only in the way they sound. If you're comparing or contrasting things, use *than,* as in *more* **than** or *less* **than.** If one thing follows or results from another, use *then* (as in, *Look,* **then** *leap*). *The next morning, Paolo was sicker* **than** *a dog. He took* *some aspirin,* **then** *went back to bed. "If gin disagrees with you,* **then** *avoid it," said Francesca.* For advice on *than* when it comes before a pronoun (*I, me, he, she,* etc.), see page 12.

though/although. These are interchangeable, except in two cases, when only *though* will do:

- in the phrases *as though* or *even though*;
- when it's used to mean "however." *Madame Olga predicted it would rain in Brazil; it didn't,* **though**.

tortuous/torturous. The first means winding, crooked, full of turns. The second, as you may suspect from its root word, *torture,* means painful. *On the* **tortuous** *drive through the mountains, Jake developed a* **torturous** *headache.*

try and/try to. The proper phrase is *try to,* as in: *"***Try to** *eat your soup without slurping," said Nancy.* But *try and* is gaining acceptance in spoken and informal use, and seems appropriate when there's an added note of defiance or stiffening of resolve: *"***Try and** *make me," said Sluggo.*

until/till. Either of these is correct, but not "til." And using *up* or *since* with *until* is unnecessary. **Until** [not *Up until*] *recently, Sluggo's tie was spotless.*

will/would. These are often confused when paired with other verbs. Use *will* after a verb in the present tense (*He* **says** *he* **will**) and *would* after a verb in the past (*He* **said** *he* **would**). For more, see page 75.

Use It (Right) or Lose It

blame. When you use *blame* as a verb (an action word), follow it with *for*, not *on*. *Lumpy **blamed** his bunions **for** the pain*. (Not: *Lumpy **blamed** the pain **on** his bunions*.) It's the bunions that are being blamed, not the pain, and *on* puts the blame where it doesn't belong!

> **NOTE:** *Putting the **blame on*** is a horse of another color. (Think of "Put the blame on Mame.") Here *blame* is a noun (a thing), not a verb; *put* is the verb, so *on* is fine.

both. The pair (of people, things, ideas, etc.) following *both* should have the same accessories:

If one has a preposition (*as, by, for, to,* and so on), so must the other: *Phineas has proposed both **to** Mary and **to** Laura*. Or: *Phineas has proposed **to** both Mary and Laura*.

If one has a verb (an action word), so must the other: *His attentions both **pleased them** and **flattered them***. Or: *His attentions were both **pleasing** and **flattering***.

comprise. It means include or contain. *Vladimir's butterfly collection **comprises** several rare specimens*. Avoid *comprised of*. You wouldn't say "included of," would you? The *of* is correct, however, in *composed of* and *consists of*.

couple. It takes *of*: *Elaine considers them a **couple of** idiots*. Not: *Elaine considers them a **couple** idiots*. Similarly, *plenty* *of, type of, variety of, breed of, kind of*: What **breed of** *dog is he?*

> **N O T E :** Sometimes *couple* is singular and sometimes it's plural. See pages 25 and 53.

d e p e n d . It takes *on.* "Well," said Buster, "that **depends on** *what* [not **depends what**] *you mean by housebroken.*"

d u e   t o . Use *due to* only if you mean "caused by" or "resulting from." Despite what some looser dictionaries allow, don't use it if you can substitute "because of" or "on account of." *The damage was **due to** moths. Richie stayed at home **because of** the hole in his suit.* Hint: If a sentence begins with *due to,* it's probably wrong, like this one: ***Due to** inclement weather, school was canceled.*

e q u a l l y   a s . Forget the *as: Ken and Midge are **equally** obnoxious.* Or: *Ken is **as** obnoxious **as** Midge.*

f o r b i d . Use *forbid* with *to,* never with *from: I **forbid** you **to** spit.* (Not: *I **forbid** you **from** spitting.*) As an alternative, you can use *forbid* with an *ing* word alone: *I **forbid** spitting.* For more about *forbid,* see page 63.

g r a d u a t e d . There are three rights and a wrong:
Right: *Moose **graduated from** college.*
Right: *Moose **was graduated from** college.*
Right: *The college **graduated** Moose.*
Wrong: *Moose **graduated** college.*

h a r d l y . Don't use *hardly* with a negative verb, as in: *She **can't hardly** see without her glasses. Hardly* is already a negative word, and you don't need two of them. Either of these is correct: *She **can hardly** see without her glasses.* Or: *She can't see without her glasses.*

hardly / scarcely / no sooner. Watch your *when*s and *than*s with these. Use *when* with *hardly* and *scarcely*: *We had **hardly** begun to cook **when** the smoke alarm went off.* Or: *We had **scarcely** begun to cook **when** the smoke alarm went off.* Use *than* with *no sooner*: ***No sooner** had we begun to cook **than** the smoke alarm went off.*

hence. Like its cousin *whence* (see below), *hence* has a built-in "from"—it means "from here" or "from now." So using "from" with *hence* is redundant. *"My birthday is three days **hence**," said Corky, "and I could really use a dehumidifier."* Another meaning of *hence* is "thus": *It's damp, **hence** the mildew.*

HIV. This is the AIDS virus; the letters stand for "human immunodeficiency virus." Since *virus* is already part of the name, it's redundant to repeat it. *He's doing research on **HIV*** (not "on the HIV virus").

inside of. Drop the *of*: *Penelope keeps her hankie **inside** her glove.*

kudos. This is a singular noun meaning praise or glory (*Bart won **kudos** for his skateboarding skill*), not a plural form of some imaginary "kudo." Show me one kudo and I'll eat it.

likely (with a verb). When you use *likely* to describe an action, don't use it all by itself; precede it with *very, quite,* or *most*: *Nathan will **quite likely** lose his shirt at the track* (not "will likely lose"). If you prefer, use *is **likely to*** instead:

Nathan is likely to lose a bundle, and Miss Adelaide is likely to kill him.

myriad. It originally meant "ten thousand," but *myriad* now means "numerous" or "a great number of." (*Lulu has myriad freckles.*) Avoid "myriads" or "a myriad of."

oblivious. It's followed by *of,* not *to. Olivia was oblivious of her liver.*

only. Aside from conversational or casual language, don't use *only* in place of *but* or *except: I would have gone to Paris, except* [not *only*] *I was broke.* For more on *only,* see page 121.

prohibit. Use *prohibit* with *from,* never with *to: The rules prohibit you from spitting.* (Not: *The rules prohibit you to spit.*) As an alternative, you can follow *prohibit* with an *ing* word alone: *The rules prohibit spitting.* For more about *prohibit,* see page 63.

whence. Not *from whence.* The "from" is built in. *Whence* means "from where." (*Go back whence you came, brigand!*) The same is true of *hence* and *thence*: use them alone, since "from" is implied. Their cousins *whither, hither,* and *thither* have "to" built in. If you must use a grizzled old word, treat it with respect. (See **hence** above.)

whether or not. You can usually ditch *or not: Phoebe knows whether Holden is telling the truth.* (See **if/whether,** page 100.)

while. The classic meaning is "during the time that": *Doc whistles while he works.* But *while* has also gained acceptance as a substitute for *although* or *whereas* at the beginning of a sentence: *While Grumpy can whistle, he prefers not to.*

NOTE: If you use *while* in place of *although,* be sure there's no chance it could be misunderstood to mean "during the time that." You could leave the impression that unlikely things were happening at the same time, as in: *While Dopey sleeps late, he enjoys vigorous exercise.* Only if Dopey is a sleepwalker! For how to use *a while* and *awhile,* see page 119.

You're Getting Warmer: Spelling and Saying It Right

accommodate. It has two *c*'s and two *m*'s. *"I believe I can accommodate you, even without a reservation,"* said Mr. Fawlty.

advertise/advertisement/advertising. Here in the United States, each of these has an *s* (the preference in Britain is to use a *z*). *When Jack got his job at the advertising agency, he didn't advertise the fact that he'd never written an advertisement.*

all-round. *Shep is a good all-round dog.* All-round is better than *all-around,* in the sense of complete or rounded. This is a case where it's better to round off the word.

arctic. Not "artic" (don't forget the middle *c*). The lower-case *arctic* means very cold. The capitalized *Arctic* means the region. And it's *Antarctica*, not "Antartica" (a common misspelling). *The Arctic expedition reached the North Pole. Next year's goal, Antarctica, is in the opposite direction.* I was astonished not long ago to see a big sign from Coors advertising a frosty beverage called Artic Ice. Never trust anything you read on the side of a bus.

artifact. Not "artefact." That's with an *i*, not an *e*: *"An 1840 saxophone is a rare artifact,"* said Lisa.

desiccated. One *s*, two *c*'s. *"A raisin is simply a desiccated grape,"* said Uncle Fester.

ecstasy. Two *s*'s (not "ecstacy"; and there's no *x*). *Kramer was in ecstasy.*

embarrass. Two *r*'s and two *s*'s. *Spock was not embarrassed by his pointy ears.*

fulfill. One *l* in the middle, two at the end. *Did Donald fulfill his obligation?*

guerrilla. Two *r*'s and two *l*'s. *Che raised a guerrilla army.*

harass. One *r* and two *s*'s. As for pronunciation, you may accent either syllable, although the preference on this side of the Atlantic is to stress the second. *"Wally, stop harassing your brother,"* said Ward.

hyperbole. It is not pronounced like a sporting event, the Hyper Bowl; it's high-PER-buh-lee. It means exaggeration or overstatement. *Buster's claim that his dog could read was hyperbole.*

NOTE: If you've seen **hyper/hypo** (page 100), you may wonder whether there's such a word as *hypobole*. As a matter of fact, there is (it means something like "suggestion"), but I've never heard anybody use it.

indispensable. It ends in *able,* not *ible.* "Nick, you're *indispensable,*" said Nora.

irresistible. It ends in *ible,* not *able.* I wish there were an easy way to tell the *ibles* from the *ables,* but there isn't. You're at the mercy of your dictionary. "Nora, you're *irresistible,*" said Nick.

judgment. No *e* after the *g.* (The same goes for *acknowledgment,* but not *knowledgeable.*) "I never make snap **judgments,**" said Solomon.

lightning. Flash! There's no *e* in *lightning,* the kind that leaves us thunderstruck: *A bolt of **lightning** split the sky.* The word with an *e* (*lightening*) comes from *lighten: I'll bet she's **lightening** her hair.*

marvelous. One *l.* (The British spell it with two, but pay no attention.) "*Gertrude, that's a **marvelous** haircut!*" said Alice.

memento. It's not spelled—or pronounced—"momento." Think of the word reme*m*brance. *The embroidered pillow was a **memento** of Niagara Falls.*

minuscule. It's not spelled—or, again, pronounced— "miniscule." Think of *minus* as the root, not *mini. Barbie's accessories are **minuscule.***

nuclear. It's pronounced NOO-klee-ur (not NOO-kyoo-lur). "*My business is **nuclear** energy,*" said Homer.

rarefied. It's spelled with one *i*, not "rarified." (If in doubt, think of *rare*.) *McCoy feared that the **rarefied** air in the* Enterprise *was enervating the crew.* (If you don't know what *enervating* means, see page 83.)

restaurateur. Notice that there's no *n* (and don't believe dictionaries that tell you there is). The root is a word meaning restore. The *restaurateur* (the person who restores you) runs the *restaurant* (where you go to get restored). *When Apu became a **restaurateur**, he called his **restaurant** Curry in a Hurry.*

skillful. Two *l*'s in the middle, one at the end. *Tex was **skillful** with a lasso.*

sprightly. The word meaning energetic has a *gh*; it's not "spritely": *Ed and Trixie were feeling **sprightly***. Someone who's like a sprite, a little imaginary creature resembling a pixie or an elf, is *spritelike*. *Ed looked **spritelike** in his leprechaun costume.*

straitjacket/straitlaced. There's no *gh* in either—not "straightjacket" or "straightlaced." ***Straitlaced** people who go over the edge may find themselves in **straitjackets***. The word *strait* is from the Latin *strictus*, which means "constricted" or "tight." *Straight,* from an Anglo-Saxon word for "stretch," means uncurved. The word you run across in geography, by the way, is *strait,* referring to a tight waterway: the *Strait* of Gibraltar, the Bering *Strait*.

toward. No final *s* ("towards"), although that's how they say it in Britain. Similarly, in American English, standard practice is not to add a final *s* to *forward, backward, up-*

ward, onward, downward, and so on. *George and Kramer were last seen heading **toward** the buffet.*

weird. It's spelled *ei,* not *ie.* *"You're looking particularly **weird** this evening, Morticia, my love," said Gomez.*

"Seedy" Endings

Words that end with a "seed" sound are notoriously hard to spell. It helps to keep in mind that all but four end with *cede.* Three end with *ceed,* and only one ends with *sede.*

- **cede:** accede, antecede, cede, concede, intercede, precede, recede, secede (and others)
- **ceed:** exceed, proceed, succeed
- **sede:** supersede

One Word or Two?

all ready/already. They're not the same. *All ready* means prepared; *already* means previously. *Becky and Darlene are all ready to boogie; in fact, they've already started.*

all together/altogether. They differ. *All together* means collectively—all at once or all in one place: *Bertie's aunts were all together in the living room.* Altogether means in sum or entirely: *Altogether there were four of them. Bertie was altogether defeated.*

any more/anymore. Use *any more* if you mean any additional; use *anymore* if you mean nowadays or any longer. *Shep won't be chasing any more cars. He doesn't get around much anymore.*

any one/anyone. If you can substitute *anybody,* then the single word *anyone* is correct; if not, use two words, *any one.* **Anyone** *can fool Lumpy.* **Any one** *of his friends is smarter than he is.* (See also **every one/everyone** below.)

anyplace. It's acceptable informally, but *anywhere* is better. *"I can't take you anyplace!" said Marge.*

anytime. One word is acceptable. *He'll take a free meal anytime.*

any way/anyway. It's one word if you mean "in any case." Otherwise, use two words, *any way.* Never "anyways." *Is there any way to visit the studio without bumping into Uma and Keanu? I'd rather see Winona, anyway.*

a while / awhile. These are often confused when they're written. *Awhile* means "for a time"; "for" is part of the meaning and shouldn't be added. *A while* means "a period of time." *Heloise rested **awhile**; she put her feet up and dozed for **a while**.* (For how to use *while,* see page 112.)

every day / everyday. We mix them up daily (or *every day*). The single word, *everyday,* is an adjective. It describes a thing, so it can usually be found right in front of a noun: *"I just love my **everyday** diamonds," said Magda.* The time expression *every day* is two words: *"That's why you wear them **every day**," said Zsa Zsa.*

every one / everyone. If you can substitute *everybody,* then the single word *everyone* is correct; if not, use two words, *every one.* ***Everyone** fears Dagmar's children. **Every one** of them is a little terror.*

Detour—Dangerous Construction Ahead

all . . . not / not all. Many sentences that are built around *all . . . not* face backward. Use *not all* instead: ***Not all** Swedes are blond.* To say, ***All** Swedes are **not** blond,* is to say that not a single Swede has golden hair.

as bad or worse than. Stay away from this kind of sentence: *Opie's math is **as bad or worse than** his English.*

Do you see what's wrong with it? Well, there are two kinds of comparisons going on, *as bad as* and *worse than.* When you telescope them into *as bad or worse than,* you lose an *as.* Putting it back in (*Opie's math is **as bad as** or **worse than** his English*) is correct but cumbersome. A better idea is to put the rear end of the comparison (*or worse*) at the end of the sentence: *Opie's math is **as bad as** his English, **or worse.*** (Another way to end the sentence is *if not worse.*)

as good or better than. This is a variation on the previous theme. It's better to split up the comparison: *Brad's haircut is **as good as** Antonio's, **or better.*** (Another way to end it is *if not better.*)

as much or more than. Here's another variation on *as bad or worse than* (see above). Don't use this phrase all at once; split it up: *Otis loves bourbon **as much as** rye, **or more.*** (Another ending is *if not more.*)

See **one of the . . . if not the** below, for a way out of another common trap.

either . . . or. Think of the elements joined by *either* and *or* as the two sides of a coin. Make sure both sides match. If what follows *either* has a subject and a verb (is a clause, in other words), what follows *or* should, too: **Either** *D.J.* **did or** *he didn't.* If what follows *either* starts with a preposition (a word that "positions," or locates, other words in the sentence), then what follows *or* should, too: *D.J. is **either** at school **or** in trouble.* If what follows *either* is an adjective (a word that characterizes something), then so is what follows *or*: *Truant officers are **either** spiteful **or***

misguided. In short, the two sides of the coin, the *either* and *or* parts, must match grammatically—subject with subject, verb with verb, preposition with preposition, adjective with adjective, and so on. If the sides don't match, you can often fix the problem by moving *either* a few words over. So this blunder, **Either** *Roseanne is angry* **or** *amused,* becomes *Roseanne is* **either** *angry* **or** *amused.*

> **NOTE:** Several other pairs should be treated as flip sides of the same coin: *neither . . . nor; not only . . . but also; both . . . and.* As with *either . . . or,* they take some arranging; all require that the two sides match.

one of the . . . if not the. Here's another corner you can avoid backing yourself into: *Jordan was* **one of the** *best,* **if not the** *best, player on the team.* Oops! Can you hear what's wrong? The sentence should read correctly even if the second half of the comparison (*if not the best*) is removed; but without it you've got: *Jordan was one of the best player on the team.* One of the best *player?* Better to put the second half of the comparison at the end of the sentence: *Jordan was* **one of the** *best players on the team,* **if not the best.**

only. This slippery word—meaning "alone," "solely," or "and no other"—can be found almost anywhere in a sentence, even where it doesn't belong. To put *only* in its place, make sure it goes right before the word or phrase you want to single out as the lone wolf. Take this sentence as an example: *The butler says he saw the murder.* By inserting *only* in various places, you can give the sentence many different meanings. Keep your eye on the underlined words—those are the wolves being singled out of the pack:

- *Only the butler says he saw the murder.* (The butler, and no one else, says he saw the murder.)
- *The butler only says he saw the murder.* (The butler says, but can't prove, he saw the murder.)
- *The butler says only he saw the murder.* (The butler says he, and no one else, saw it.)
- *The butler says he only saw the murder.* (He saw—but didn't hear—the murder.)
- *The butler says he saw only the murder.* (He saw just the murder, and nothing else.)

Remember: *Only* the lonely! It's easy to slip *only* into a sentence carelessly, so get into the habit of using it right in front of the word you want to single out.

N O T E : The whole point of putting *only* in its place is to make yourself understood. In the examples above, the various locations of *only* make a big difference. But in informal writing and conversation, if no one's likely to mistake your meaning, it's fine to put *only* where it seems most natural—usually in front of the verb: *I'm only going to say this once; This food can only be called swill.* The more grammatically correct versions—*I'm*

*going to say this **only** once; This food can be called **only***
swill—only sound unnatural.

reason . . . is because. Here's a redundancy for you,
a wording that seems to repeat itself: *The **reason** Ned*
*stayed home **is because** robbers tied him up.* Can you hear
the echo effect? *Because* means "for the reason that," so the
example says, in effect: *The **reason** Ned stayed home is **for***
***the reason that** robbers tied him up.* Use one or the other,
not both: *The **reason** Ned stayed home is that robbers tied*
him up. Or: *Ned stayed home **because** robbers tied him up.*

Overwriters Anonymous

at this time. A bit overstuffed, no? (*The doctor has no*
*openings **at this time**.*) Why not just *now*? (*The doctor has*
no openings now.)

if and when. Wordy people are very fond of this phrase
(*I'll punch out his lights, **if and when** I see him*). Use either
if or *when*; you seldom need both.

in order to. Unless there's some need for special emphasis, drop *in order* and simply use *to*: "*I work **to** live, and*
*I live **to** boogie*," said Tallulah.

unless or until. ("*I'm not talking, **unless or until** I see*
my lawyer!" *said Mr. Bluster.*) One or the other will usually
do, unless or until you're getting paid by the word.

Sensibility and Sense

chair. I admit I'm fighting a losing battle on this one. Many people now use *chair* as a verb—*Mr. Gekko **chaired** the meeting*—inspired, perhaps, by the precedent of *table* as a parliamentary term. You will also find *chair* being used as a noun by people who want to avoid saying *chairman* or *chairwoman*. (In some circles, for all I know, you may be able to table the chair.) Personally, I prefer *chair* as an article of furniture. But I'm afraid that people called *chairs* will continue to *chair* for years to come, especially on university campuses and in the halls of government. This is a matter of taste. I've made my choice in this game of musical *chairs;* you must make yours.

gender. Let's hope *gender* never replaces *sex*. An old and durable word, *sex* (from the Latin *sexus*) has long meant either of the two divisions—male and female—characterizing living things. (*Annie Oakley was a credit to her sex*.) By extension it has also come to refer to the sexual act. *Gender,* a grammatical term for "kind," describes the ways some languages categorize nouns and pronouns by sex (masculine, feminine, or neuter). Perhaps it was inevitable that as we began speaking more openly about sex and sex roles, some people would feel a need for a more neutral word to refer to the Great Divide, one with no taint of the act itself. *Gender* seemed to fit the bill. (*Lit-*

*tle Emily plays with dolls of both **genders**.*) Well, this horse, too, is out of the barn. But to my ear, *gender* sounds prudish as an alternative to *sex*. Until a better word comes along, I'll stick with the three-letter original. If *sex* was good enough for Jane Austen ("Miss de Bourgh is far superior to the handsomest of her sex"), it's good enough for me.

Department of Hot Air

dialogue. Can we *dialogue*? No. But we can talk, chat, gossip, speak, converse, exchange ideas, or shoot the breeze. Some people would prefer to *dialogue,* or to *have a dialogue.* Don't talk to them. (For a related cliché, see **meaningful dialogue**, page 174.)

impact. The kind of person who uses language as a sledgehammer is likely to use *impact* as a verb meaning affect. (*"The third-quarter loss will **impact** our earnings projections for the year," said Daddy Warbucks.*) If you don't want to give the rest of the world a headache, use *impact* only as a noun. (*"Will this have any **impact** on my allowance?" asked Annie.*)

interface. People who like to *dialogue* also like to *interface.* By this they mean interact, or work together. Don't work with them.

Call Me E-Mail

Attention, techno-weenies. Stop littering the info highway. Don't call a grammatical time-out when you log on. English is English, whether it comes over the phone, via the Postal Service (excuse me, "snail mail"), or on the Internet.

Let's clean up cyberspace, gang. You wouldn't use *pls* for *please, yr* for *your,* or *thnx* for *thanks* in a courteous letter. So why do it on the Net? You don't shout or whisper on the telephone. So why use ALL CAPITAL or all lowercase letters in your E-mail? Making yourself hard to read is bad "netiquette."

And another thing. IMHO (in my humble opinion), those abbreviations like CUL (see you later) and BTW (by the way) are overused. You're too busy for full sentences? So what are you doing with the time you're saving by using cute shortcuts? Volunteering at your local hospital? Sure. I'm ROFL (rolling on floor laughing).

You digerati can speak E-lingo among yourselves, but try real English if you want the cyber-impaired to get it. Next time you log on, remember there's a person at the other end, not a motherboard. Use appropriate grammar and punctuation. Be clear and to the point. And consider phoning once in a while.

monies. This is how a bureaucrat says *money*. *"But where will these monies come from?" asked Councilman Windbag.*

paradigm. It masquerades as a two-dollar word, but it's really worth only about twenty cents. A *paradigm* (the *g* is silent; PAIR-a-dime) is simply a pattern or example. It's not a standard of perfection (that's a *paragon*). Still, homely old *paradigm* (along with its relatives *paradigmatic,* pair-a-dig-MAT-ic, and *paradigmatically*) has become the darling of those who like to dress up ordinary ideas in technicalities. *"Our ad campaign has a paradigmatic resonance," said Mr. Palaver.*

parameter. There's nothing like a scientific word to lend an air of authority to a weak sentence. *("Let us review the parameters of the issue," said Senator Blowhard.)* That's how a word like *parameter* (a mathematical term for a type of arbitrary constant or independent variable) worms its way into the Official Overwriters' Vocabulary. Don't let it get into yours. *Parameters* are not boundaries—those are *perimeters*—and neither are they characteristics, elements, parts, components, qualities, requirements, or features. Unless you know an independent variable from an arbitrary constant, stay away from *parameter*.

say. You've *said* it before, and you'll *say* it again, because if there's a word that *says* it all, surely it's the verb *say*. *("I love you," he said.)* So why do some writers avoid it? The problem with *say* is that it's just too simple and clear and straightforward for many people. Why *say* something, when you can declare, assert, expostulate, whine, exclaim, groan, peal, breathe, cry, explain, or asseverate it? I'm all for variety and freshness of expression, but let's not go overboard. As Freud said, sometimes a cigar is just a cigar.

transpire. This is how a stuffed shirt says *happen* or *occur* or *take place*: *"Let us review exactly what **transpired** at the First Continental Congress,"* said Professor Jawbone.

unprecedented. *Judge Hearsay's action was **unprecedented**.* Oh yeah? Very few things are unprecedented. Don't use this word to mean unusual, uncommon, odd, unexpected, rare, exceptional, curious, irregular, offbeat, or surprising. No matter how extraordinary something sounds to you, there's probably a precedent for it. *Mr. Scrooge's generosity was **unprecedented**—for him.*

You Call That a Word?

ahold. A horror! Either it's two words (*"Gal, you've really got **a hold** on me,"* said Roy), or it's simply *hold* (*"For heaven's sake, Roy, get **hold** of yourself,"* said Dale).

ain't. It's still misbehavin'. Not: *"I **ain't** hanging up my six-guns just yet,"* said Shane.

alot. Ouch! It's two words: *a lot. He hasn't done his friends **a lot** of good.*

alright. No, *alright* is not *all right*—it's all wrong! *"**All right**, I'll let you whitewash the fence!"* said Tom.

anywheres. Never. It's *anywhere. "The aliens could be almost **anywhere**,"* said Ripley.

being that. This clunker is sometimes used as an alternative to *since* or *because*: ***Being that** he was hungry, he ate a piece of Mildred's fruitcake*. It may squeak by in conversation (not with me, please!) but should be avoided in writing. *Being as* and *being as how* are just as bad. They aren't felonies, but neither is snoring at the ballet. (The same goes for *seeing that, seeing as,* and *seeing as how*.)

complected. No; the word is *complexioned*. *After years of riding the range with no sunscreen, Yosemite Sam was dark-complexioned*.

dove (for **dived**). *Dived* is still the preferred past tense for what Esther Williams did off a diving board, but *dove* is surfacing more and more. In writing, stick to *dived*; in conversation, especially if it's casual, you can get by with *dove* (though I'd rather see it sink). *With the swamp before him and an angry rhino at his heels, Indiana **dived** into the murky waters*.

irregardless. This isn't a word—it's a crime in progress! The word you want is *regardless*. (*Dick and Nicole do as they like, **regardless** of the consequences*.) Irrespective of what you hear and read, there is no such word as *irregardless*.

orientate. The extra syllable is ugly and unnecessary, though not a hanging offense. *Orient* is sufficient. *Santiago tried to **orient** himself without a compass*.

preventative. The extra syllable isn't wrong, but it's unnecessary. Use *preventive*. *Always wear sunscreen as a **preventive** measure*.

seeing that. See **being that** above.

Et Cetera

an. Sometimes it's the little things that give us away—for instance, whether to use *a* or *an* before words beginning with *h* or *u*. Here's a pair of handy rules:

- Use *a* (not *an*) in front of words that start with these sounds: a "sounded" *h* (the *ha-ha* variety, as in *history, horror, hotel*); a "long" *u* (the *yew* variety, as in *university, utopia, eulogy, European*).
- Use *an* in front of words that start with these sounds: a "silent" *h* (*hour, honor, herbal*); a "short" *u* (*uncle, umbrella, umber*).

and/or. This ugly wrinkle (*Tubby, would you like apple pie and/or ice cream?*) can be smoothed out: *Tubby, would you like apple pie, ice cream, or both?*

but. It's common practice to use *but* to mean *nothing but* or *only*—just be careful not to get tangled in negatives, since *but* in these cases already has a negative sense built in. *Tom **is but** a boy.* Not: *Tom **isn't but** a boy.*

*Aunt Polly **weighs but** 105 pounds.* Not: *Aunt Polly **doesn't weigh but** 105 pounds.*

> **NOTE:** Avoid using *help but*, as in: *Huck **can't help but** look silly in those pants.* Drop the *but* and use the *ing* form: *Huck **can't help** looking silly in those pants.*

etc. Since this abbreviation (it stands for *et cetera*) means *and others*, it's redundant to say or write "and etc." It's even worse to use "etc., etc." (*A conscientious groupie knows all the members of a band: drummer, lead guitar, rhythm, bass, etc.*) And by the way, if you're one of those people who pronounce it ek-SET-ra, shame on you. There's no *k* sound.

Chapter 6

Comma Sutra

The Joy of Punctuation

An editor I know at *The New York Times* once received a gift from a writer friend. It was the tip of a lead pencil, broken off and wrapped up and presented along with a card that said, "A gross of commas, to be used liberally throughout the year as needed." Now, that writer understood the gift of punctuation!

When you talk, your voice, with its pauses, stresses, rises, and falls, shows how you intend your words to fit together. When you write, punctuation marks are the road signs (stop, go, yield, slow, detour) that guide the reader, and you wouldn't be understood without them.

If you don't believe me, try making sense out of this pile of words:

Who do you think I saw the other day the Dalai Lama said my Aunt Minnie.

There are at least two possibilities:

- *"Who do you think I saw the other day?" the Dalai Lama said. "My Aunt Minnie."*
- *"Who do you think I saw the other day? The Dalai Lama!" said my Aunt Minnie.*

(I know, I know. I've taken liberties with *who* and *whom*. You can, too. See the chapter on pronouns, page 9.)

Punctuation isn't some subtle, arcane concept that's hard to manage and probably won't make much of a difference one way or another. It's not subtle, it's not difficult, and it can make all the difference in the world.

The Living End: The Period (.)

The period is the red light at the end of a sentence. When you reach the period, it's all over. Whatever thought you were trying to convey has been delivered. A straightforward sentence that states rather than asks or exclaims something starts with a capital letter and ends with a period.

But what if there's a dot there already, as when a sentence ends with an ellipsis (. . .) or an abbreviation (M.D., for example)? And what if a sentence has a smaller sentence within it? Here's what you do:

• If a sentence ends with an abbreviation, don't add a final period: *As a new immigrant, Apu's nephew felt welcome in the U.S.*

• If a sentence ends in an ellipsis (three dots that indicate an omission), put a period first to show that the sentence is over: *"You'd like to borrow fifty dollars?" said Apu. He recalled the old saying, Neither a borrower nor a lender be. . . .*

But if you want to emphasize a deliberate trailing off, you may omit the period. End the sentence with a space, then the three dots: *"Well . . ."*

• If a sentence concludes with the title of a work that ends in a question mark or an exclamation point, don't add a final period: *Liz gained twenty pounds for* Who's Afraid of Virginia Woolf? *We couldn't get seats to* Oklahoma!

• If a sentence has a smaller sentence within it (surrounded by dashes or parentheses), don't use a period to end the "inside" sentence: *When Apu made him an offer—"I could use some help around the store"—he accepted.*

NOTE: This last point doesn't apply to question marks or exclamation points: *Apu criticized his nephew's manners ("Speak up! How are the customers supposed to hear you?") and his grooming ("Do you call that a beard?").*

U n c o m m o n l y   U s e f u l :
T h e   C o m m a   (,)

There's nothing much to punctuating a sentence, really, beyond a little comma sense. Get the commas right, and the
rest will fall into place.

Yeah, yeah, I hear you saying. What's a comma or two—or
three? How can something so small, so innocuous, be important? Well, that attitude can get you tossed into grammatical
purgatory. You don't believe it? Take a look:

Cora claimed Frank planned the murder.

Without commas, the finger of guilt points to Frank. But
add a pair of commas, and Cora becomes the suspect:

Cora, claimed Frank, planned the murder.

Here's another pair of examples with completely different
meanings:

Augie quit saying he was looking for another job.

Augie quit, saying he was looking for another job.

In the first sentence, Augie quit talking; in the second, he
quit his job.

The lesson: Don't take commas for granted. They're like
yellow traffic lights. If you ignore one, you could be in for a
bumpy ride.

Most problems with commas have to do with dividing a
sentence into parts—larger parts like clauses (each with its
own subject and verb), or smaller ones like items in a series.
Commas are also used to interrupt a sentence and insert an-

other thought. Here's how to get out of some of the most common comma complications.

Long and Short Division

● Use a comma to separate big chunks (clauses) of a sentence with *and* between them. *Tina hadn't left the city in months, and by Friday she was climbing the walls.* If there's no *and* in between, use a semicolon instead: *Tina hadn't left the city in months; by Friday she was climbing the walls.*

● Use commas to separate a series of things or actions. *She packed a toothbrush, a blow-dryer, her swimsuit, and her teddy bear. She finished packing, paid some bills, ate a few Oreos, and watered the plants.*

NOTE: The final comma in those two series, the one just before *and,* can be left out. It's a matter of taste. But since its absence can sometimes change your meaning, and since there's no harm in leaving it in, my advice is to stick with using the final comma.

As I Was Saying

● Use commas before and after the names of people you're talking to: *"Good-bye, Mom. Dad, be good,"* she said, *and hung up the phone.* You can skip the comma before the name if all that precedes it is *and* (*"And Mom, don't worry"*) or *but* (*"But Dad, you promised"*).

- Use commas before or after a quotation: *"Let's see,"* *said Tina.* Or: *Tina said, "Let's see."* But don't use a comma after a quotation that ends with an exclamation point or a question mark: *"Have I forgotten anything?" she wondered. "Sunscreen!" she exclaimed.*

Let Me Interrupt

- Use a comma after an introductory phrase if a pause is intended: *As usual, she checked to make sure the stove was turned off. Of course, it always was. You see, Tina was a bit compulsive.*
- Use commas around an aside—information that could just as well go in parentheses: *Her upstairs neighbor, the one without the tattoos, promised to collect her mail.*
- Use commas around *which* clauses: *The airport bus, which was usually on time, never came. So she took a taxi, which cost her an arm and a leg.*

But don't use commas around *that* clauses: *The bus that she had planned to take never came, so she grabbed the first taxi that she saw.*

For more on *which* and *that,* see page 3.

Semi-Avoidance: The Unloved Semicolon (;)

The semicolon is one of the most useful but least used punctuation marks. For whatever reason, many of us avoid it. Maybe it intimidates us; it shouldn't. (See, wasn't that easy?) If a comma is a yellow light and a period is a red light, the semicolon is a flashing red—one of those lights you drive through after a brief pause. It's for times when you want something stronger than a comma but not quite so final as a period. Here's when to use it.

- Use a semicolon to separate clauses when there's no *and* in between: *Andy's toupee flew off his head; it sailed into the distance.*
- Use semicolons to separate items in a series when there's already a comma in one or more of the items: *Fred's favorite things were his robe, a yellow chenille number from Barneys; his slippers; his overstuffed chair, which had once been his father's; murder mysteries, especially those by Sue Grafton; and single-malt Scotch.*

✳ Let Me Introduce You:
The Colon (:)

Think of the colon as a traffic cop, or punctuation's master of ceremonies. Use it to present something: a statement, a series, a quotation, or instructions. But remember that a colon is an abrupt stop, almost like a period. Use one only if you want your sentence to brake completely. Keep these guidelines in mind.

- Use a colon instead of a comma, if you wish, to introduce a quotation. *I said to him: "Harry, please pick up a bottle of wine on your way over. But don't be obsessive about it."* Many people prefer to introduce a longer quotation with a colon instead of a comma.
- Use a colon to introduce a list, if what comes before the colon could be a small sentence in itself (it has both a subject and a verb). *Harry brought three wines: a Bordeaux, a Beaujolais, and a Burgundy.*
- Don't use a colon to separate a verb from the rest of the sentence, as this example does. *In Harry's shopping bag were: a Bordeaux, a Beaujolais, and a Burgundy.* If you don't need a colon, why use one? *In Harry's shopping bag were a Bordeaux, a Beaujolais, and a Burgundy.*

NOTE: If what comes after the colon is a complete sentence, start it with a capital letter. *My advice was this: Bring only one next time.*

Huh?
The Question Mark (?)

The question mark is the raised eyebrow at the end of a sentence. It's used with a question, of course, but also to show skepticism or surprise. (*"Lost? My luggage got lost on a direct flight?"*) Here are some of the most common questions about questions.

● What do you do when a sentence has a series of questions? This gets an either/or answer.

You can put the question mark at the very end: *Would Nina have to buy a new hair dryer, toothbrush, swimsuit, camera?*

Or, for emphasis, you can put a question mark after each item (you don't need capital letters for each item, since it's still one sentence): *Would Nina have to buy a new hair dryer? toothbrush? swimsuit? camera?*

● How do you introduce a question within a longer sentence? The simplest way is to use a comma and start the question with a capital letter. *The question was, How long should she wait for her luggage?*

The same is true if the question is a quotation: Introduce it with a comma. *Nina cried, "What next?"*

But if the introduction is a complete sentence, especially if it's a long one, a colon works better. *The question she asked herself was this: How long should she wait for her baggage?*

• What comes after a question mark? If the sentence continues after the question, don't use a comma after the question mark. *What will I do without my hair dryer? she asked herself.* "*What more can go wrong?" she said to the ticket agent.*

The Silent Scream: The Exclamation Point (!)

The exclamation point is like the horn on your car—use it only when you have to. A chorus of exclamation points says two things about your writing: First, you're not confident that what you're saying is important, so you need bells and whistles to get attention. Second, you don't know a really startling idea when you see one.

When you do use an exclamation point, remember this:

• Use it alone (don't add a comma afterward): "*Holy cow!" said Phil.*

And keep your voice down.

A Brief Interlude:
Parentheses ( )

Once in a while you may need an aside, a gentle interruption to tuck information into a sentence or between sentences. One way to enclose this interruption is with parentheses (the end rhymes with *breeze*), and you just now saw a pair.

The thing to know about parentheses is that they can enclose a whole sentence standing alone, or something within a sentence. The tricky part is determining where the other punctuation marks go: inside or outside the closing parenthesis. Punctuation never precedes an opening parenthesis.

- When the aside is a separate sentence, put punctuation inside the parentheses, and start with a capital letter: *Jimmy thinks he has won the lottery. (He is mistaken, however.)*
- When the aside is within a sentence, put punctuation outside the parentheses, and start with a small letter. *Jimmy thinks he has won the lottery (he's mistaken).*

An exception occurs when the remark inside parentheses is an exclamation (*wow!*) or a question (*huh?*). The exclamation point or question mark goes inside the parentheses, but any other punctuation marks go outside: *Jimmy has already made plans for the money (poor guy!), but his wife is skeptical. He may have misread the numbers on his lottery tickets (how dumb can you get?).*

Too Much of a Good Thing:
The Dash (—)

We could do with fewer dashes. In fact, the dash is probably even more overused these days than the exclamation point—and I admit to being an offender myself (there I go again).

The dash is like a detour; it interrupts the sentence and inserts another thought. A single dash can be used in place of a colon to emphatically present some piece of information: *It was what she dreaded most—fallen arches.* Or dashes can be used in pairs instead of parentheses to enclose an aside or an explanation: *Her shoes had loads of style—they were Ferragamos—but not much arch support.*

Dashes thrive in weak writing, because when thoughts are confused, it's easier to stick in a lot of dashes than to organize a smoother sentence. Whenever you are tempted to use dashes, remember this:

- Use no more than two per sentence. And if you do use two, they should act like parentheses to isolate a remark from the rest of the sentence: *After the flight, Nina looked—and she'd be the first to admit it—like an unmade bed.*
- If the gentler and less intrusive parentheses would work as well, use them instead. *Nina's luggage (complete with her return ticket) appeared to be lost.*

By the way, don't confuse the dash with the hyphen (see below). The dash is longer. If you want a dash but your computer keyboard doesn't have one, use two hyphens (--).

Betwixt and Between: The Hyphen (-)

A hyphen is not just a stubby version of the dash. The two of them do very different things. While the dash separates ideas or big chunks in a sentence, the hyphen separates (or connects, depending on how you look at it) individual words or parts of words: *My mother-in-law works for a quasi-official corporation that does two-thirds of its business with the government.*

When a word breaks off at the end of a line in your newspaper and continues on the next line, a hyphen is what links the syllables together. But the kind of hyphen most of us have problems with is the one that goes (or doesn't go) between words, as in terms for some family members (*mother-in-law*), or in two-word descriptions (*quasi-official*), or in fractions (*two-thirds*). Here are some guidelines for when you need a hyphen and when you don't.

The Part-time Hyphen

One of the hardest things to figure out with hyphens is how to use them in two-word descriptions. When two words are combined to describe a noun, sometimes you use a hyphen between them and sometimes you don't.

The first question to ask yourself is whether the description comes before or after the noun.

- If it's after the noun, don't use a hyphen: *Father is strong willed. My cousin is red haired. This chicken is well done.* Ducks are *water resistant.*
- If it's before the noun, use a hyphen when either of the two words in the description wouldn't make very much sense by itself. *He's a strong-willed father. I have a red-haired cousin. This is well-done chicken. Those are water-resistant ducks.*

Exceptional Situations

Here are some exceptions to the "before or after" rule for hyphens in two-word descriptions:

- If *self* or *quasi* is one of the words, always use a hyphen: *Robert is self-effacing; still, he's a self-confident person. He's our quasi-official leader; the position is only quasi-legal.*
- If both words could be used separately and still make sense, don't use a hyphen even if they come before a

noun: *Phoebe is a **naughty old** cat. Alicia is a **sweet young** thing.*

- If *very* is one of the two words, forget the hyphen: *That Hepplewhite is a **very expensive** chair.* If *very* is added to a description that would ordinarily take a hyphen (***much-admired** architect,* for example), drop the hyphen: *Sam's a **very much admired** architect.*

- If one of the two words ends in *ly,* you almost never need a hyphen: *That's a **radically different** haircut. It gives you an **entirely new** look.*

- If one of the words is *most, least,* or *less,* leave out the hyphen: *The **least likely** choice, and the **less costly** one, is the **most preposterous** hat I've ever seen.*

Is Your Hyphen Showing?

Here are some cases where you must use hyphens:

- With *ex* (meaning "former"). *Hal is the **ex-president** of the company.*

- When adding a beginning or an ending to a word that starts with a capital (*anti-British, Trollope-like*). Two exceptions are *Christlike* and *Antichrist.*

- When adding *like* would create a double or triple *l* (*shell-like*).

- When adding a beginning or ending would create a double vowel (*ultra-average, anti-isolationist*). But *pre* and *re* are often exceptions to this (*preempt, reexamine*), so when you have a duplicate vowel, look up the word in the dictionary. (The vowels are *a, e, i, o, u*.)

● With fractions. ***Three-quarters*** *of the brownies and* ***two-thirds*** *of the cookies are gone.* For how to go halves, see below.

Half Measures

I wish there were a rule for *half*, but it's all over the map. Some formations involving *half* are one word (*halfhearted, halfway*), some are two words (*half note, half sister*), and some are hyphenated (*half-hour, half-moon*). Check the dictionary.

HEADS OR TAILS

Many of us can't add a beginning or an ending to a word without sticking in a hyphen for good measure. If we put *mini* in front of *van*, it inexplicably becomes *mini-van* instead of *minivan*; if we put *like* after *life*, it unaccountably becomes *life-like*, not *lifelike*. Many hyphens show up where they're not wanted. Here are some common endings and beginnings that don't usually need them:

Endings

ache: I'll trade my **toothache** for your **headache**.

less and *most:* The **ageless** soprano can still hit the **uppermost** notes.

like: What a **lifelike** Gainsborough.

wide: Sewer rats are a **citywide** menace.

Beginnings

anti: Samson was **antifeminist**.

bi: They're conducting a **bicoastal** romance.

co: This celebrity autobiography has no **coauthor**.

extra: His **extracurricular** schedule is full.

inter: Luke has **intergalactic** ambitions.

micro, mini, and *multi:* Excuse me for a moment while I **micromanage** a **minicrisis** among these **multitalented** children.

mid: Our raft sank **midstream**.

non: Hubert is a **nonperson**.

over and *under:* Be **overcautious** if your date is legally **underage**.

post: He lives in a **postwar** building.

pre and *pro:* The **prenuptial** atmosphere was definitely **promarriage**. (See NOTE below.)

re: They have **reexamined** their situation. (See NOTE below.)

semi: I wish I'd invented the **semiconductor**.

sub and *super:* Our **subbasement** got **supersaturated** in the flood.

Hyphens in the Family

Some family members get hyphens and some don't. Here's how to keep them straight.

USE A HYPHEN

- With *ex.* Meet my **ex-husband**.
- With *in-law.* Fred's my **brother-in-law**.
- With *great.* There goes my **great-aunt**.

DON'T USE A HYPHEN

- With *step.* His **stepson** Charlie is a doctor.
- With *half.* Bob's **half brother** is a thug.
- With *grand.* She can't be a **grandmother**!

trans: Leslie is a **transsexual**.
ultra: That Nancy is **ultrachic**.
un: Argyle socks with sneakers are **uncool**.

NOTE: There are exceptions, cases when you'll want to use a hyphen in words starting with *pre, pro,* and *re*. If a word starting with *pre* or *pro* is just too hard to read without a hyphen, add one (*pre-iron, pro-choice*). And if a word starting with *re* could be confused with one that's spelled the same but means something else, add a hyphen. For instance, use *re-cover* (for "cover again") to avoid confusion with the word *recover*. Other examples include *re-creation, re-petition, re-press, re-sent, re-serve, re-sign, re-sort, re-treat.* (When the boss asks to renew your employment contract, it makes a big difference whether you reply in your memo, "I'm going to re-sign" or "I'm going to resign.")

A Multitalented Mark: The Apostrophe (')

That little airborne mark that dangles over some words (including last names like O'Conner) is called an apostrophe. This is the punctuation mark that has many sign painters mystified. Store awnings and windows, sides of trucks, even neon signs, are peppered with wayward apostrophes that either don't belong at all or are in the wrong position. Beware, especially, of the unusual apostrophe in a plural word.

Here's how to use an apostrophe with . . .

• **Possessives.** To indicate ownership, add *'s* to a singular noun or to a plural noun that does not end in *s*: **Buster's** *bulldog has wrecked the* **children's** *room.* Add the apostrophe alone to a plural noun that ends in *s*:

This was the boys' idea. (Chapter 3 is all about posses-sives, in case you need to know more.)

● **Some unusual plurals.** Add *'s* to make plurals of numbers and letters, including abbreviations: *Libby, the daughter of two CPA's, was born in the 1940's, and earned all B's at Swarthmore.* When a number is written out, it gets no apostrophe: *She spent **millions** of dollars in **tens** and **twenties**.*

● **Missing letters.** An apostrophe can show where let-ters have been dropped in a shortened word or phrase. For example, *shouldn't* is short for *should not;* the apos-trophe shows where the *o* in *not* was dropped. Some other clipped words are quite irregular, like *won't* and the illegitimate *ain't.* Shortened words and phrases are called contractions; there's a list of them on pages 73–74 (they're also in the dictionary). When in doubt, look it up.

● **A comma or period.** When you need a comma or pe-riod (or any other punctuation, for that matter) after a possessive word that ends with an apostrophe, the punctuation goes after the apostrophe: *The idea was the **boys**', but the responsibility was their **parents**'.*

Enough Said:
Quotation Marks (" ")

Think of quotation marks as bookends that support a quotation in between.

The opening quotation marks always go right before the first word of the quotation: *"Can we talk?"* The trick is at the other end, where the closing quotation marks go. You'll have to decide whether the punctuation that follows the quoted material (period, comma, question mark, or whatever) goes inside or outside the closing quotation marks. Here's what's in and what's out.

The Ins

- **Period.** *"I think I'm going to be sick."*
- **Comma.** *"I shouldn't have eaten those strawberries,"* Gustav said.

The Outs

- **Colon.** *There are two reasons she hates the nickname "honey": It's sticky and it's sweet.*
- **Semicolon.** *Frank's favorite song is "My Way"; he's recorded it several times.*

Sometimes In, Sometimes Out

- **Question mark.** In most cases, a question mark should be inside the quotation marks: *"Who goes there?" said the sentry. "What is the password?"* But the question mark must be outside if it's not part of the actual quotation: *Who starred in "Dynasty"?*

- **Exclamation point.** In most cases, an exclamation point goes inside the quotation marks: *"Captain!" said Sulu. "We're losing speed!"* But the exclamation point goes outside if it's not part of the quotation: *My God, the screen just went blank after reading "Situation Normal"!*

- **Parentheses.** If the entire quotation is in parentheses, then the closing parenthesis should go outside the quotation marks: *Uhura had the last word ("I told you so").* If only part of the quotation is in parentheses, then the closing parenthesis goes inside the quotation marks: *She added, "Maybe next time you'll listen to me (if there is a next time)."*

- **Apostrophe.** How do we get ourselves into messes like this one? To create the possessive of something that's normally in quotation marks—for example, the title of a poem, "The Raven"—you would have to put the apostrophe outside: *"The Raven"'s first stanza is the best.* Pretty awful-looking, isn't it? It's so awful that many publications even cheat to avoid it, and write *"The Raven's"*—definitely incorrect, although much prettier. My advice is to avoid this problem entirely. Instead of writing *"The Raven"'s author was Poe,* rearrange it: *Poe was the author of "The Raven."*

NOTE: When one quotation appears within another, enclose the interior one in single quotation marks: *"Was it Linus who said, 'Get lost'?" asked Lucy.*

The Slant on Titles

You may have wondered why some titles, like *Vogue* and *Huckleberry Finn,* most often appear in the slanting letters called italics, while others, like "Bedroom at Arles" and "My Funny Valentine," usually appear in ordinary type surrounded by quotation marks.

Customs vary on how titles should be written. In most newspaper writing, for example, all titles are in plain type, though not all go inside quotation marks.

My advice is to follow conventional practice. Put the names of larger works, like books, movies, and plays (and magazines and newspapers), in italics. Put the names of smaller works, like poems, stories, and paintings, in ordinary type with quotation marks.

Use Italics

Books: *Gone With the Wind*
Magazines: *Newsweek*
Newspapers: *The Miami Herald*
Movies: *Million Dollar Legs*

The Less Said:
When Not to Quote

Sign painters seem to love quotation marks. They don't care how a word is spelled, as long as it's enclosed in quotes. I don't know much about the sign-painting business—maybe they get paid extra for punctuation. Here are a few signs of the times I've spotted lately:

Nail salon: *Our Instruments Are "Sterilized"*
Pizzeria: *"Free" Delivery*
Locksmith: *"Fast" and "Friendly" Service*

There's no reason for quotation marks in any of those signs. The intent may be to emphasize the quoted words, but a bright color or a different typeface would do a better job.

In fact, quotation marks used like that can mislead the reader. They're sometimes used in a skeptical or sarcastic way, to indicate that what's quoted isn't meant seriously: *Uncle Oscar's regular Friday-night "volunteer work" turned out to be a poker game.*

The moral is: Don't quote it if you don't have to. And the next time your pipes spring a leak and a truck marked *"Licensed" Plumber* pulls up to your door, don't say I didn't warn you.

Plays, musicals, operas, ballets: *Macbeth, Guys and Dolls, The Magic Flute, Swan Lake*

Use Quotation Marks

Articles: "The Cellulite Cure: Fact or Fiction?"

Essays: "Civil Disobedience," by Henry David Thoreau

Poems: "The Raven," by Edgar Allan Poe

Short stories: "The Secret Life of Walter Mitty," by James Thurber

Paintings, sculptures: "Nude Descending a Staircase," "Venus de Milo"

TV series: "Jeopardy!"

Song titles: "Begin the Beguine"

NOTE: Where titles are concerned, classical music has its own variations on the theme. Here, too, usage varies widely. I recommend writing the formal names of symphonies, concertos, sonatas, and similar compositions in ordinary type without quotation marks: Mahler's Symphony No. 2 in C Minor, Mozart's Serenade in D. But if you use a nickname, put it in quotation marks: Beethoven's "Emperor" Concerto, Schubert's "Trout" Quintet.

Chapter 7

The Compleat Dangler

A Fish out of Water

Life would be pretty dull if everyone's English were perfect. Without slips of the tongue, we wouldn't have spoonerisms, the tongue-tanglers named after the befuddled Reverend William A. Spooner. He was the Victorian clergyman who spoke of "Kinquering Congs" and greeted someone with, "I remember your name perfectly, but I just can't think of your face."

And we wouldn't have malapropisms, either. Mrs. Malaprop was a character in an eighteenth-century play whose bungled attempts at erudite speech led her to declare one gentleman "the very pineapple of politeness!" and to say of another, "Illiterate him . . . from your memory."

We're lucky that English, with its stretchy grammar and its giant grab-bag of a vocabulary, gives us so much room for verbal play, if not anarchy. As Groucho Marx said, "Love flies out the door when money comes innuendo," and it's hard to imagine him saying it in Esperanto.

Naturally, if you have room to play, you have room to make mistakes. And English sentences are often constructed without regard for building codes. I've grown almost fond of one common error, the dangler. It's a word or phrase (a group of words) that's in the wrong place at the wrong time, so it ends up describing the wrong thing. Here comes one now: *Strolling along the trail, Mount Rushmore came into view.* The opening phrase, *strolling along the trail,* is a dangler. Why? Because it's attached to the wrong thing, *Mount Rushmore.* The way the sentence stands, the mountain was out taking a stroll!

Danglers show up in newspapers and best-sellers, on the network news and highway billboards, and they can be endlessly entertaining—as long as they're perpetrated by someone else. When you're doing the talking or writing, the scrambled sentence isn't so amusing. See if you can tell what's wrong with these examples.

- *Born at the age of forty-three, the baby was a great comfort to Mrs. Wooster.* As the sentence is arranged, the baby—not his mother—was forty-three. (The opening phrase, *born at the age of forty-three,* is attached to *the baby,* so that's what it describes.) Here's one way to rearrange things: *The baby, born when Mrs. Wooster was forty-three, was a great comfort to her.*

- *Tail wagging merrily, Bertie took the dog for a walk.* See how *tail wagging merrily* is attached to *Bertie?* Put the tail on the dog: *Tail wagging merrily, the dog went for a walk with Bertie.*

- *As a den mother, Mrs. Glossop's station wagon was always full of Cub Scouts.* Whoa! The phrase *as a den mother* is attached to *Mrs. Glossop's station wagon.* Attach it to the lady herself: *As a den mother, Mrs. Glossop always had her station wagon full of Cub Scouts.*

Danglers are like mushrooms in the woods—they're hard to see at first, but once you get the hang of it they're easy to find. Although the wild dangler may lurk almost anywhere in a sentence, the seasoned hunter will look in the most obvious place, right at the beginning of the sentence. If the first phrase is hitched to the wrong wagon—or no wagon at all—it's a dangler. Some kinds of opening phrases are more likely than others to be out of place. I'll show you what to look for.

THE USUAL SUSPECT

Always suspect an *ing* word of dangling if it's near the front of a sentence; consider it guilty until proved innocent. To find the culprit, ask yourself whodunit. Who's doing the *walking, talking, singing,* or whatever? You may be surprised by the answer. In these examples, look at the phrase containing the *ing* word and look at whodunit.

- *After overeating, the hammock looked pretty good to Archie.* Who ate too much in this sentence? The hammock! If a person did the overeating, the opening *ing* phrase should be attached to him: *After overeating, **Archie** thought the hammock looked pretty good.*

- *On returning home, Maxine's phone rang.* Who came home? Maxine's phone! To show that the owner of the phone was doing the returning, put her right after the opening phrase: *On returning home, **Maxine** heard the phone ring.*

- *Walking briskly, the belt of her raincoat was lost.* Who's the pedestrian? The belt! What's attached to the opening phrase is what's doing the walking. If you want to say *she* was walking briskly, put her right after the opening phrase: *Walking briskly, **she** lost the belt of her raincoat.*

Pin the Tail on the Donkey

Have you ever seen children at parties pinning the tail on the wrong part of the donkey? Well, sometimes adjectives (words that characterize nouns) get pinned to the wrong part of a sentence and become danglers. Here's a sentence with its "tail" in the wrong place:

Incorrect: ***Dumpy and overweight**, the vet says our dog needs more exercise.*

The description *dumpy and overweight* should be pinned on the dog, not the vet:

Correct: **Dumpy and overweight**, *our dog needs more exercise, the vet says.* A more graceful solution would be to rewrite the sentence completely: *The vet says our dog needs more exercise because she's* **dumpy and overweight**.

Adjectives (such as *dumpy* and *overweight*) like to be pinned on the nearest noun.

HITCH YOUR WAGON

A dangling adverb at the front of a sentence is a lot like a horse that's hitched to the wrong wagon. Adverbs (words that characterize verbs) can be easy to spot because they often end in *ly*. When you see one, make sure it's "hitched" to the right verb. In this example, what went wrong at the hitching post?

Incorrect: **Miraculously** *we watched as the surgeon operated with a plastic spoon.*

As the sentence stands, the opening word, *miraculously,* refers to the watching, not the operating. That's because the closest verb is *watched.* To fix things, put the *ly* word closer to the right action:

Correct: **Miraculously**, *the surgeon operated with a plastic spoon as we watched.*

Here's another solution: *We watched as the surgeon* **miraculously** *operated with a plastic spoon.*

Adverbs (such as *miraculously*) like to be hitched to the nearest verb.

ROADS TO NOWHERE

You can easily be led astray when a sentence has a road sign at the very beginning. The kind of sign I mean is a preposition, a word that shows position or direction (*at, by, on, with,* and so on). If the sign is in the wrong place, you end up on the road to nowhere. Try to avoid this kind of dangler:

Incorrect: **At the age of ten,** *my father bought me a puppy.*

As the sentence is written, Dad was only a boy! That's because the opening phrase, *at the age of ten,* is attached to *my father*—an obvious mismatch. If the sign is to point in the right direction, the sentence has to be rearranged:

Correct: **At the age of ten,** *I got a puppy from my father.*

Or: *My father bought me a puppy* **when I was ten.**

TO'S A CROWD

Some of the hardest danglers to see begin with *to.* A sentence that starts with an infinitive (a verb form usually preceded by *to,* for instance *to run, to see, to build*) can't be left to dangle. The opening phrase has to be attached to whoever or whatever is performing the action. Here's an opening phrase that leaves the sentence scrambled:

Incorrect: **To crack an egg properly,** *the yolk is left intact.*

As the sentence is written, the yolk is the one cracking the egg. The opening phrase, *to crack an egg properly,* is attached to *the yolk,* not to whoever is doing the cracking. Let's put a cook in the kitchen.

Exceptions That Make the Rule

Some expressions are so common that they're allowed to dangle at the beginning of a sentence, even though they're not connected to anything in particular. We treat them as casually as throat-clearing. For example, we may say: **Generally speaking**, *pigeons mate for life*. The pigeons aren't the ones doing the speaking, naturally, and no one would make such a connection. Other stock phrases that can dangle to their hearts' content include *strictly speaking, barring unforeseen circumstances, considering the alternative, assuming the worst, judging by appearances, after all, by and large, on the whole, admittedly, put simply, given the conditions, in the long run, in the final analysis, to tell the truth, contrary to popular belief,* and *to be perfectly frank.* Introductory phrases like these have become so familiar that they have earned the right to be exceptions to the rule.

Correct: *To crack an egg properly, you must leave the yolk intact.*

Here's an even simpler way to say it: *To crack an egg properly, leave the yolk intact.* (The subject is understood to be *you.* This is called an imperative sentence, since someone's being told to do something.)

Owners' manuals, you'll notice, are chock-full of dangling infinitives. Does this sound familiar? *To activate widget A, doohickey B is inserted into slot C.* If the one trying to activate the silly thing is *you,* make *you* the subject: *To activate widget A, you insert doohickey B into slot C.* Or you can delete the *you,* since it's understood to be the subject: *To activate widget A, insert doohickey B into slot C.*

A LIKELY STORY

Looking for a dangler? Then look for a sentence that starts with *like* or *unlike.* More than likely, you'll find a boo-boo. Here's a likely candidate.

Incorrect: *Like Alice, Fran's nose job cost plenty.*

The phrase *like Alice* is a dangler because it's attached to the wrong thing: *Fran's nose job.* Presumably Fran, and not her nose job, is *like* Alice. Make sure the things being compared really are comparable. There are two ways to fix a sentence like this.

Correct: *Like Alice, Fran paid plenty for her nose job.* Or: *Like Alice's, Fran's nose job cost plenty.*

Chapter 8

Death Sentence

Do Clichés Deserve to Die?

Tallulah Bankhead once described herself as "pure as the driven slush." And bankruptcy has been called "a fate worse than debt." We smile at expressions like these out of relief, because we're braced for the numbing cliché that fails to arrive.

Nothing is wrong with using a figure of speech, an expression that employs words in imaginative (or "figurative") ways to throw in a little vividness or surprise. But it's an irony of human communication that the more beautiful or lively or effective the figure of speech, the more likely it will be loved, remembered, repeated, worn out, and finally worked to death. That's why some people will tell you that the Bible and Shakespeare are full of clichés!

So crowded is our stock of figurative language that every

profession—legal, corporate, fashion, artistic, and literary, among others—seems to have a collection all its own. A tired book critic, for example, will say a novel is "a richly woven tapestry," "a tour de force," or "a cautionary tale," one whose characters are either "coming of age" or experiencing "rites of passage." For corporate "high rollers," the "bottom line" is what matters, whether a company is "in play" or its stock has "gone south."

Then are all clichés and familiar turns of phrase to be summarily executed? No. Let your ear be your guide. If a phrase sounds expressive and lively and nothing else will do, fine. If it sounds flat, be merciless. One more point. It's far better to trot out a dependable cliché, and to use it as is, than to deck it out with lame variations (*the tip of the proverbial iceberg*) or to get it wrong ("unchartered seas" instead of *uncharted* ones; "high dungeon" instead of *dudgeon*). And two unrelated figures of speech shouldn't be used one after the other, whether they're clichés or not (*He got off his high horse and went back to the drawing board*). That's called mixing your metaphors, and there's more about it at the end of this chapter.

There's no way to eliminate all clichés. It would take a roomful of Shakespeares to replace them with fresh figures of speech, and before long those would become clichés, too. Vivid language is recycled precisely because it's vivid. But think of clichés as condiments, the familiar ketchup, mustard, and relish of language. Use when appropriate, and don't use too much. When you're dressing up a hamburger, you don't use béarnaise sauce. You use ketchup, and that's as it should be. But you don't put it on everything. Some dishes, after all, call for something special. Here are some of today's more overworked "condiments."

Acid test. Overuse and you flunk.

Agree to disagree. People never really *agree to disagree.* They just get tired of arguing.

Back to the drawing board. Back to *Roget's Thesaurus.*

The ball is in your court. Only if you're Andre Agassi.

Beat a dead horse. Anyone who uses this expression more than once a month should be required to send a donation to the ASPCA.

Bite the bullet. Save your teeth.

Bitter end. This is right up there with *making ends meet.*

Blanket of snow. Nature is a *fertile field* (there's another one) for clichés. Besides *blankets of snow,* beware *sheets of rain, calms before the storm, devastating earthquakes, raging torrents, bolts from the blue, steaming jungles, uncharted seas* (which are likely to become *watery graves*), *wide-open spaces, places in the sun,* and anything *silhouetted against the sky.* (See also *golf-ball-sized hail* below.)

Blessing in disguise. Not disguised well enough.

Boggles the mind. It's all right to be boggled once in a while, but don't make a habit of it.

Bone of contention. This expression is getting osteoporosis.

Bored to tears. There has to be a more exciting way to complain of boredom.

Bottom line. Unless—and even if—you're talking about finance, there's probably a better way to say it.

Broad daylight. The sun has begun to set on this one, and on *light of day.*

Brute force. This phrase is no longer forceful.

A bug going around. Another way of saying you don't know what you've got.

By hook or by crook. This one hangs out in the same crowd with *hook, line, and sinker* and *lock, stock, and barrel.*

Can of worms. Don't open this one too often. And don't unnecessarily disturb its cousins, *nest of vipers* and *hornet's nest.*

Can't see the forest for the trees. If you find yourself using this expression over and over again, you have a myopic imagination.

Champing at the bit. If you must use it, get it straight. Restless horses *champ* at their bits; they don't "chomp."

Come to a head. Sometimes seen as *bring to a head,* this phrase has its humble beginnings in dermatology. Need I say more?

Cool as a cucumber. Using this too much is uncool.

Cutting edge. It's no longer sharp.

Days are numbered. A phrase that's not just overused, but depressing.

Dead as a doornail. Why a doornail, anyway? (Also see *passed away* below).

Diamond in the rough. And watch those *pearls before swine,* too. When accessorizing your language, remember that a little jewelry goes a long way.

Discreet silence. Silence makes good clichés (*eloquent silence, chilly silence*). And in the silence, of course, you can *hear a pin drop.*

Draw a blank. This is what you do when you run out of clichés.

Each and every. The resort of a weak writer, like *one and the same* and *any and all.*

Easier said than done. What isn't? As for *no sooner said than done,* it's a promise that's seldom kept.

Errand of mercy. The truly merciful don't resort to clichés.

Far be it from me. When you say this, you're about to butt in where you don't belong. If you do want to be a buttinsky, though, use it correctly (not "far be it for me").

Fell through the cracks. An unconvincing way of saying something is not your fault. And don't make it worse by saying "fell between the cracks."

Few and far between. This is what fresh expressions are becoming.

Food for thought. I'd say this expression is *from hunger,* but that's another cliché.

Fools rush in. And when they get there, they use clichés.

Foregone conclusion. A pedestrian way of saying that something was no surprise.

Foreseeable future. The future is not foreseeable. Anyone who knows otherwise should be in the commodities market.

Generation gap. An even worse cliché, *Generation X,* has already become geriatric.

Get nowhere fast. It's a cliché, all right, but it's better than *spinning your wheels.*

Get the show on the road. This expression closed in New Haven.

Glass ceiling. This phrase, like *level playing field,* is getting tired. Wouldn't you like to give it some time off?

Golf-ball-sized hail. Why golf balls? How about plums or Ping-Pong balls for a change?

Grind to a halt. OK, you can use this maybe once a year.

Head over heels. I've never understood this one. Wouldn't *heels over head* make more sense?

Heated argument. Go easy on this expression. What better kind of argument is there, after all?

His own worst enemy. Not unless he badmouths himself behind his back.

Impenetrable fog. Maybe we should bring back *thick as pea soup.*

In the nick of time. "Just in time" isn't good enough?

Innocent bystander. Why is a *bystander* always *innocent*? Has anybody given him a lie-detector test?

It goes without saying. Then don't say it.

Last but not least. If it's not least, then don't put it last.

Leaps and bounds. Gazelles and antelopes, and maybe even lizards, move by *leaps and bounds;* few other things do.

Legendary. This and *fabled* are much overused. What legend? What fable? Unless you're Aesop or the Brothers Grimm, give these words a vacation.

Make a killing. The best thing to be said about this cliché is that it's better than being *taken to the cleaners.* Don't use either of them to excess.

Mass exodus. As opposed to an exodus of one? In most cases, *exodus* alone is enough.

Meaningful dialogue. This was a dumb expression to begin with. Drop *meaningful.* In fact, *dialogue* is pretty dumb, too. Don't people have talks anymore?

Moment of truth. Ever notice that it's always bad news?

More than meets the eye. If you've got a good eye, there's not that much more.

Nip it in the bud. This nipping of buds has to stop.

Pandora's box. Put a lid on it.

Passed away. You've probably noticed that death is a favorite playground of clichés. This is too bad. In situations where people most need sincerity, what do they get? Denial. There's no shame in saying somebody died, but the vocabulary of mortality avoids it. Think again before using expressions like *passed away* or *passed on* (sometimes reduced to just *passed*), *untimely end, cut down in his prime, called to his Maker, called away, great beyond, this mortal coil, bought the farm, kicked the bucket, gone to a better place, checked out, grim reaper, in the midst of life, irreparable loss, broke the mold, vale of tears, time heals all, words can't express, tower of strength,* or *he looks like he's sleeping.*

Play hardball. This expression seems to have edged out *no more Mr. Nice Guy.* But it's not as intimidating as it once was, so why not give it a rest?

Play it by ear. This is a nice old image. Let's not wear it out, except at the piano.

Political hopefuls. I vote no.

Powers that be. This is much overused by powers that wannabe.

Pre-existing condition. This has an authoritative sound, but it's a redundancy (that means it repeats itself, like *end result, final outcome, new initiative,* and *close proximity*).

Pushing the envelope. Isn't it amazing how fast a new phrase gets old? Like *A-OK,* this one is starting to get quaint.

Reliable source. Are your other sources lying scoundrels?

Roller coaster. This phrase (usually preceded by some descriptive term like *emotional* or *fiscal*) comes up a lot in news stories about natural disasters, crippling illness, the federal budget, or the Olympic Games. Let's hope the ride will soon be over.

Sadder but wiser. Some people are *sadder but wiser* after hearing *a word to the wise.* These are nice old expressions that could be with us for a long time if they're treated gently, but *only time will tell.*

Sea of faces. These are often *bright and shining faces.* Commencement speakers, why not give these expressions a sabbatical?

Seat of the pants. And very shiny pants they are. Let's not wear them out.

Seriously consider. This isn't just hackneyed, it's insincere. If someone tells you he'll *seriously consider* your suggestion, he's already kissed it off. That goes double if he has promised to give it *active* or *due consideration.*

Shattered with grief. Why does this phrase make us think of insincere widows?

Sickening thud. This was a lively image in the first five thousand mystery novels where it appeared. The *sickening thud* usually came after *a shot rang out.*

Tarnished image. The *tarnished image* (distantly related to the old *blot on the escutcheon*) could use some polishing. Give it a leave of absence.

Team player. When your boss says you should be more of a *team player,* that means she wants you to take on more of her work.

Thick as thieves. Thieves are not that thick, anyway. Otherwise, plea bargaining would never work.

Tip of the iceberg. A *tip of the hat* to anyone who can come up with something better.

To the manner born. If you're going to use a cliché, respect it. This Shakespearean phrase (it comes from *Hamlet*) means "accustomed to" or "familiar with." It is not "to the manor born" and has nothing to do with aristocracy.

Tongue in cheek. The only expression more trite than *tongue in cheek* is *tongue firmly in cheek.* I wish we could retire both of them.

Trust implicitly. Never believe anybody who says you can trust him implicitly.

Tumultuous applause. Really? Applauding, even enthusiastically, is pretty gratifying to the guy onstage. Throwing tomatoes is tumultuous.

Up in the air. Let's come up with a more *down-to-earth* way of saying this.

Viable alternative. Well, it beats the alternative that doesn't work.

War-torn. This cliché stays alive because, regrettably, there are always enough wars to go around. Anything that's *war-torn,* by the way, is bound to be *embattled* or *besieged.*

What makes him tick. This image is winding down. Don't overdo it.

Metaphors Be with You

Is it any wonder we love figures of speech? Just think how dull language would be without them. The metaphor, the most common figure of speech, lets us use one image—any image we want!—to conjure up another. Imagination is the only limit. This gives us about a zillion ways (give or take a few) of saying the same thing.

The phrase *volley of abuse*, for example, uses the image of a fusillade of bullets to describe an outpouring of anger. This metaphor leaves behind a single vivid picture.

But if that image has to compete with another (as in, *The volley of abuse was the straw that broke the camel's back*), we have what's called a mixed metaphor. No clear picture emerges, just two dueling ideas (bullets versus straws). If you've heard it's unwise to mix metaphors, this is why: The competing images drown each other out, as in, *the silver lining at the end of the tunnel*, or *Don't count your chickens till the cows come home*.

Some people are so wild about metaphors that they can't resist using them in pairs. This may work, if the images don't clash: *Frieda viewed her marriage as a tight ship, but Lorenzo was plotting a mutiny.* Since the images of *tight ship* and *mutiny* have an idea in common (sailing), they blend into one picture. But usually when two figures of speech appear together, they aren't so compatible. In that case, the less said, the better.

Chapter 9

The Living Dead

Let Bygone Rules Be Gone

The house of grammar has many rooms, and some of them are haunted. Despite the best efforts of grammatical exorcists, the ghosts of dead rules and the spirits of imaginary taboos are still rattling and thumping about the old place.

Sometimes an ancient prohibition becomes outdated, or it may turn out that a musty convention was never really a rule at all. The trouble is that these phantoms are hard to displace, once they take hold in our minds. It's no longer considered a crime to split an infinitive or end a sentence with a preposition, for example, but the specters of worn-out rules have a way of coming back to haunt us. In the interest of laying a few to rest, I dedicate to each a tombstone, complete with burial service. May they rest in peace.

TOMBSTONE: Don't split an infinitive.

R.I.P. An infinitive is a verb in its simplest form, right out of the box. It can usually be recognized by the word *to* in front of it: *Blackbeard helped him to escape.* But the *to* isn't actually part of the infinitive and isn't always necessary: *Blackbeard helped him escape.* As a preposition, a word that positions other words, the *to* lets us know an infinitive is coming.

The truth is that the phrase "split infinitive" is misleading. Since *to* isn't really part of the infinitive, there's nothing to split. A sentence often sounds better when the *to* is close to the infinitive: *Violet decided to ask for a raise.* But there's no harm in separating them by putting a descriptive word or two in between: *Violet decided **to bravely ask** for a raise.* Just don't go overboard. Not: *Violet decided **to for the first time ever and without even blinking ask** for a raise.*

Writers of English have been merrily "splitting" infinitives since the 1300's, and it was considered acceptable until the mid–nineteenth century, when grammar books—notably Henry Alford's *Plea for the Queen's English*—started calling it a crime. (Some linguists trace the taboo to the Victorians' slavish fondness for Latin, a language in which you *can't* divide an infinitive.) This "rule" was popular for half a century, until leading grammarians debunked it. But its ghost has proved more durable than Freddy Krueger.

TOMBSTONE: It's wrong to end a sentence with a preposition.

R.I.P. Here's another bugaboo that English teachers used to get worked up *over*.

We can blame an eighteenth-century English clergyman named Robert Lowth for this one. He wrote the first grammar book to say that a preposition (a positioning word, like *at, by, for, into, off, on, out, over, to, under, up, with*) shouldn't go at the end of a sentence. This idea caught on, even though great literature from Chaucer to Shakespeare to Milton is bristling with sentences ending in prepositions. Nobody knows why the notion stuck—possibly because it's closer to Latin grammar, or perhaps because the word *preposition* means "position before," which seems to suggest that a preposition can't come last.

At any rate, this is a rule that modern grammarians have tried to get us out from under.

TOMBSTONE: *Data* is a plural noun and always takes a plural verb.

R.I.P. It's time to admit that *data* has joined *agenda, erotica, insignia, opera,* and other technically plural Latin and Greek words that have become thoroughly Anglicized as singular nouns taking singular verbs. No plural form is necessary, and the old singular form, *datum,* can be left to the Romans. (*Media,* it seems, is going the same way, though it's not there yet. Ask me again in a few years.)

TOMBSTONE: Always put the subject of a sentence before the verb.

R.I.P. Says who? Tell it to Tennyson (*"Into the valley of Death / Rode the six hundred"*). He didn't mind putting his subject (*the six hundred*) after the verb (*rode*).

True, most of the time a sentence with its subject (the one doing the action) before the verb (the action being done) sounds more forceful and direct than one written the other way around. *Frank came later* has more oomph than *Later came Frank.* But every now and then it's appropriate to put the verb first (*Says who?* for instance), and literature is full of poetic examples of verbs preceding their subjects. (Just ask Poe: *"Quoth the Raven, 'Nevermore.'"*)

> **NOTE:** If a sentence starts with *there,* its real subject probably follows the verb, as in: *There was a young man from Darjeeling.* (The subject isn't *there;* it's *man.*) Sentences starting with *there* get a bad rap in many grammar guides. There's nothing wrong with them, either. See page 55.

TOMBSTONE: It's wrong to start a sentence with *and* or *but.*

R.I.P. But why's it wrong? There's no law against occasionally using *and* or *but* to begin a sentence.

Over the years, some English teachers have enforced the notion that *and* and *but* should be used only to join elements within a sentence, not to join one sentence with another. Not so. It's been common practice to begin sentences with them since at least as far back as the tenth century. But don't overdo it, or your writing will sound monotonous.

 **TOMBSTONE:** Don't split the parts of a verb phrase (like *has been*).

R.I.P. This has never been a rule. It's a by-product of the famous superstition about splitting an infinitive (see the first tombstone, page 182).

 **TOMBSTONE:** *None* is always singular.

R.I.P. Not always. In fact, *none* is more likely to be plural.

Many people seem to have been taught (mistakenly) that *none* always means "not one" (as in, **None** *of the chickens* **is** *hatched*). But most authorities have always believed that *none* is closer in meaning to "not any (of them)" than to "not one (of them)." So it's considered plural in most cases and takes a plural verb: **None** *of the chickens* **are** *hatched.*

None is singular only when it means "none of it"—that is to say, "no amount." (**None** *of the milk* **was** *spilled.*)

If you really do mean "not one," say "not one." (There's more about *none* in the chapter on plurals, page 27.)

✳   ✳   ✳

TOMBSTONE: Only living things can form the possessive with *'s*.

R.I.P. According to this musty old custom, you wouldn't say *the piano's leg* (you'd make it *the leg of the piano*), or *the house's roof* (you'd say *the roof of the house*). Apparently, inanimate things aren't as possessive as living ones. Silly, right? Well, this *book's* position is that *yesterday's* custom can be safely ignored.

There's nothing wrong with using *whose* to refer to inanimate objects, either: *Never buy a **house whose roof** leaks or a **piano whose leg** is wobbly.*

TOMBSTONE: Use *It is I*, not *It is me*.

R.I.P. Here's another ordinance that's out of date. It's OK to use *It is me, That's him, It's her*, and similar constructions, instead of the grammatically correct but more stuffy *It is I, That's he*, and *It's she*.

Similarly, it's fine to say *Me too*. The alternative, *I too*, is still grammatically correct, but unless you're addressing the Supreme Court or the Philological Society, you can drop the formality.

There's more about *I* and *me* on page 11.

TOMBSTONE: Don't use *who* when the rules call for *whom*.

R.I.P. We can't dump *whom* entirely, at least not just yet. But many modern grammarians believe that in conversation or informal writing, *who* is acceptable in place of *whom* at the beginning of a sentence or clause (a clause is a group of words with its own subject and verb): **Who's** *the package for? You'll never guess* **who** *I ran into the other day.*

Where *whom* should be used after a preposition (*to, from, behind, on,* etc.), you can substitute *who* in casual situations by reversing the order and putting *who* in front. *"From* **whom***?"* becomes *"***Who** *from?"*

There's a more detailed discussion of *who* versus *whom* on pages 5–10.

TOMBSTONE: Always use an active verb (*Bonnie* **drove** *the getaway car*) and avoid a passive one (*The getaway car* **was driven** *by Bonnie*).

R.I.P. It's true that a passive verb makes for a more wimpy, roundabout way of saying something. The more straightforward way is to put the one performing the action (*Bonnie*) ahead of the one being acted upon (*the getaway car*), with the verb in between: subject . . . verb . . . object.

But the direct way isn't always the best way. The passive might be more appropriate in cases like these:

• When there's a punch line. You might want to place the one performing the action at the end of the sentence for emphasis or surprise: *The gold medal in the five-hundred-meter one-man bobsled competition* **has been won** *by a six-year-old child!*

- When nobody cares whodunit. Sometimes the one performing the action isn't even mentioned: *Hermione* **has been arrested**. *Witherspoon* **is being treated** *for a gunshot wound*. We don't need to know who put the cuffs on Hermione, or who's stitching up Witherspoon.

TOMBSTONE: Never use a double negative.

R.I.P. My advice on double negatives: "Never say never."

The double negative wasn't always a no-no. For centuries, it was fine to pile one negative on top of another in the same sentence. Chaucer and Shakespeare did this all the time to accentuate the negative. It wasn't until the eighteenth century that the double negative was declared a sin against the King's English, on the ground that one negative canceled the other. (Blame the clergyman and grammarian Robert Lowth, the same guy who decided we shouldn't put a preposition at the end of a sentence.)

As for now, stay away from the most flagrant examples (*I didn't do nothing; You never take me nowhere*), but don't write off the double negative completely. It's handy when you want to avoid coming right out and saying something: *Your blind date is* **not unattractive**. *I* **wouldn't** *say I* **don't** *like your new haircut*. (There's more on double negatives in the glossary.)

TOMBSTONE: Use *I shall* instead of *I will*.

R.I.P. Once upon a time, refined folk always used *I shall* or *we shall* to refer to the simple future, not *I will* or *we* *will*. But *will* has edged out *shall* as the people's choice. *Shall* can still be used with *I* and *we* in an offer or a proposal: **Shall I** *freshen your drink, or* **shall we** *go?*

There's more about the demise of *shall* in the chapter on verbs (page 71).

TOMBSTONE: You can't *hold* a meeting and you can't *throw* a party.

R.I.P. Baloney. I've done it myself.

Once in a while you'll hear someone (probably an editor) say that Councilman Windbag *convenes* or *conducts* a meeting, he doesn't *hold* one; or that the Venables *give* a party, they don't *throw* one.

Prohibitions like these confuse literalness with precision. The fact is that metaphors—figures of speech, like *My car is a lemon*—have an exactness all their own. If the Venables' party was a real blast, they *threw* it. If they hired a string quartet and served cucumber sandwiches, they *gave* it.

Metaphors are fine as long as they're appropriate, but beware of two kinds: the metaphor that's worn out (see the chapter on clichés), and the metaphor that's "mixed," or has too many images, as in, *This lemon is my Achilles' heel.* (There's more about mixed metaphors on pages 178–179.)

TOMBSTONE: Use *more than* instead of *over*.

R.I.P. You may have been told by some pedant that *over* doesn't apply to numbers, only to quantities. Not so. It's fine to use *over* in place of *more than* or *in excess of*: *Dad's new car gets **over** ten miles to the gallon.*

TOMBSTONE: Don't use *since* to mean "because."

R.I.P. Now and then, an extremely conservative grammarian will suggest that *since* should be used only to indicate a time period (*since Thursday,* for example). Forget that, if you ever heard it. *Since* doesn't always mean "from the time that." It can also mean "because" or "for the reason that." (***Since** you asked me, I'll tell you.*) People have been using *since* in this way for five hundred years.

Just be sure the meaning can't be confused, as in, ***Since** we spoke, I've had second thoughts.* In that case, *since* could mean either "from the time" or "because," so it's better to be more precise.

TOMBSTONE: Don't use *while* to mean "although."

R.I.P. Some grammarians believe that *while,* which comes from an Anglo-Saxon word meaning "time," should be used only to mean "during the time that."

But there's a long tradition, going back at least to the sixteenth century, of using *while* at the head of a sentence to mean "although" or "whereas": ***While** he may be short, he's wiry.*

Just be sure the meaning can't be confused, as in: ***While** he reads the* Times, *he watches the news on CNN.* In this case, *while* could mean either "during the time that" or "although." Pick one of those and avoid the confusion.

One more thing about *while*. Some people overuse it as a way to vary their sentences and avoid using *and*. Let's not wear out a useful word for no good reason. If *while* isn't meant, don't use it. Not: *Wally wears suspenders,* **while** *his favorite shoes are wingtips.*

TOMBSTONE: Use *lighted*, not *lit*.

R.I.P. There's nothing wrong with using *lit* for the past tense of *light*: *Paul **lit** two cigarettes, then gave one to Bette.*

TOMBSTONE: Use *have got*, not *have gotten*.

R.I.P. People who take this prohibition seriously have gotten their grammar wrong.

At one time, everyone agreed that the verb *get* had two past participles: *got* and *gotten*. (The past participle is the form of a verb that's used with *have, had,* or *has.*) It's true that the British stopped using *have gotten* about three hundred years ago, while we in the Colonies kept using both *have got* and *have gotten*. But the result is not that Americans speak improper English. The result is that we have retained a nuance of meaning that the unfortunate Britons have lost.

When we say, *Bruce **has got** three Armani suits,* we mean he has them in his possession. It's another way of saying he *has* them.

When we say, *Bruce **has gotten** three Armani suits,* we mean he's acquired or obtained them.

It's a useful distinction, and one that the British would do well to reacquire.

TOMBSTONE: Drop the *of* in *all of* and *both of*.

R.I.P. Some members of the Redundancy Police think *of* is undesirable in the phrases *all of* and *both of,* except in front of a pronoun (*all of me, both of them,* etc.). They frown on sentences like **Both of** the thieves spent **all of** the money, and would prefer **Both** the thieves spent **all** the money.

Either way is correct. There's no law against keeping *of,* but by all means drop it if you want to. You can't please all of the people all the time.

TOMBSTONE: Use *as . . . as* for positive comparisons, and *so . . . as* for negative ones. For example: *She's* **as old as** *Fran, but* **not so old as** *you.*

R.I.P. Not so fast! For centuries, it's been correct to use *as . . . as* in positive comparisons (*as fat as ever*) and to use either *as . . . as* or *so . . . as* in negative comparisons (*not as fat as before, not so fat as all that*). If you want to use *so . . . as* in a negative comparison, go right ahead. But *as . . . as* is correct in all cases.

If anyone tries to tell you otherwise, just remind him that in Old English, both *as* and *so* (*eall* and *swa*) appeared in the same word, *ealswa.* It was used in comparisons eight or more centuries ago pretty much the way we use *as* these days (*ealswa good ealswa gold*).

TOMBSTONE: Don't start a sentence with *there*.

R.I.P. There is no doubt that a statement starting with *there* begins on a weak note. It's weak because *there* is a phantom subject, standing in for the real one. *There is a party going on* is a different way of saying, *A party is going on.* The real subject in both cases is *party.*

Some English teachers frown on starting a sentence with *there* (possibly because they prefer keeping the real subject before the verb). Never mind. There's nothing wrong with it. In fact, literature is full of splendid examples: *"There is a tide in the affairs of men, which, taken at the flood, leads on to fortune."*

Chapter 10

Saying Is Believing

How to Write What You Mean

A good writer is one you can read without breaking a sweat. If you want a workout, you don't lift a book—you lift weights. Yet we're brainwashed to believe that the more brilliant the writer, the tougher the going.

The truth is that the reader is always right. Chances are, if something you're reading doesn't make sense, it's not your fault—it's the writer's. And if something you write doesn't get your point across, it's probably not the reader's fault—it's yours. Too many readers are intimidated and humbled by what they can't understand, and in some cases that's precisely the effect the writer is after. But confusion is not complexity; it's just confusion. A venerable tradition, dating back to the ancient Greek orators, teaches that if you don't know what you're talking about, just ratchet up the level of difficulty and no one will ever know.

Don't confuse simplicity, though, with simplemindedness. A good writer can express an extremely complicated idea clearly and make the job look effortless. But such simplicity is a difficult thing to achieve, because to be clear in your writing you have to be clear in your thinking. This is why the simplest and clearest writing has the greatest power to delight, surprise, inform, and move the reader. You can't have this kind of shared understanding if writer and reader are in an adversary relationship.

Now, let's assume you know what you want to say, and the idea in your head is as clear as a mountain stream. (I'm allowed a cliché once in a while.) How can you avoid muddying it up when you put it into words?

There are no rules for graceful writing, at least not in the sense that there are rules for grammar and punctuation. Some writing manuals will tell you to write short sentences, or to cut out adjectives and adverbs. I disagree. The object isn't to simulate an android. When a sentence sounds nice, reads well, and is easy to follow, its length is just right. But when a sentence is lousy, you can take steps to make it more presentable. These are general principles, and you won't want to follow all of them all of the time (though it's not a bad idea).

1. Say what you have to say.

Unless you're standing at a lectern addressing an audience, there's no need to clear your throat. Your listeners aren't finding their seats, putting down their forks, wrapping up a conversation, or whatever. Your audience—the reader—is ready. So get to it.

These are the kinds of throat-clearing phrases you can usually ditch:

At this juncture I thought you might be interested in knowing . . .

Perhaps it would be valuable as we arrive at this point in time to recall . . .

I can assure you that I'm sincere when I say . . .

In light of recent developments the possibility exists that . . .

(Of course, some messages could do with a bit of cushioning: *We at the bank feel that under the circumstances you would want us to bring to your attention as soon as possible the fact that . . . your account is overdrawn.*)

2. Stop when you've said it.

Sometimes, especially when you're on a roll and coming up with your best stuff, it's hard to let go of a sentence (this one, for example), so when you get to the logical end you just keep going, and even though you know the reader's eyes are glazing over, you stretch one sentence thinner and thinner—with a semicolon here, a *however* or *nevertheless* there—and you end up stringing together a whole paragraph's worth of ideas before you finally realize it's all over and you're getting writer's cramp and you have to break down and use a period.

When it's time to start another sentence, start another sentence.

How do you know when it's time? Well, try breathing along with your sentences. Allow yourself one nice inhalation and exhalation per sentence as you silently read along. If you start to turn blue before getting to the end, either you're reading too slowly (don't move your lips) or the sentence is too long.

3. Don't belabor the obvious.

Some writers can't make a point without poking you in the ribs with it. A voice isn't just pleasing; it's pleasing *to the ear.* You don't just give something away; you give it away *for free.* The reader will get the point without the unnecessary prepositional phrases (phrases that start with words like *by, for, in, of,* and *to*): pretty *in appearance,* tall *of stature,* blue *in color,* small *in size,* stocky *in build,* plan *in advance,* drive *by car,* assemble *in a group.* You get the picture.

4. Don't tie yourself in knots to avoid repeating a word.

It's better to repeat a word that fits than to stick in a clumsy substitute that doesn't. Just because you've called something a spider once doesn't mean that the next time you have to call it an arachnid or a predaceous eight-legged creepy-crawly.

Editors sometimes call this attempt at elegant variation the Slender Yellow Fruit Syndrome. It is best explained by example: *Freddie was offered an apple and a banana, and he chose the slender yellow fruit.*

5. Be direct.

Too many writers back into what they have to say. A straightforward statement like *He didn't intend to ruin your flower bed* comes out *His intention was not to ruin your flower bed.*

Don't mince words. If what you mean is, *Mom reorganized my closet brilliantly,* don't water it down by saying, *Mom's reorganization of my closet was brilliant.*

Here are a couple of other examples:

Their house was destroyed in 1993. Not: *The destruction of their house occurred in 1993.*

We concluded that Roger's an idiot. Not: *Our conclusion was that Roger's an idiot.*

If you have something to say, be direct about it. As in geometry, the shortest distance between two points is a straight line.

6. Don't make yourself the center of the universe.

Of course we want to know what happened to you. Of course we care what you think and feel and do and say. But you can tell us without making every other word *I* or *me* or *my.* (Letter writers, who are fast becoming an endangered species, are often guilty of this. Next time you write a letter or memo, look it over and see how many sentences start with *I*.)

You can prune phrases like *I think that,* or *in my opinion,* or *let me emphasize that* out of your writing (and your talking, for that matter) without losing anything. Anecdotes can be told, advice given, opinions opined, all with a lot fewer first-person pronouns than you think.

This doesn't mean we don't love you.

7. Put descriptions close to what they describe.

A television journalist in Iowa once said this about a suspected outbreak of hoof-and-mouth disease: *The pasture contained several cows seen by news reporters that were either diseased or dying.*

Do you see what's wrong? The words *diseased or dying* are supposed to describe the cows, but they're so far from home that they seem to describe the reporters. What the journalist should have said was: *Reporters saw a pasture containing several cows that were either diseased or dying.*

When a description strays too far, the sentence becomes awkward and hard to read. Here's an adjective (*bare*) that has strayed too far from the noun (*cupboard*) it describes: *Ms. Hubbard found her **cupboard**, although she'd gone shopping only a few hours before, **bare**.* Here's one way to rewrite it: *Although she'd gone shopping only a few hours before, Ms. Hubbard found her **cupboard bare**.*

And here's an adverb (*definitely*) that's strayed too far from its verb (*is suing*): She **definitely**, *if you can believe what all the papers are reporting and what everyone is saying*, **is suing**. Put them closer together: *She **is definitely suing**, if you can believe what all the papers are reporting and what everyone is saying.*

The reader shouldn't need a map to follow a sentence.

8. Put the doer closer to what's being done.

Nobody's saying that sentences can't be complex and interesting; they can, as long as they're easy to follow. But we shouldn't have to read a sentence twice to get it. Here are a couple that take us from Omaha to Sioux City by way of Pittsburgh:

*The **twins**, who had gone to the same schools and camps all their lives despite the advice of their parents and teachers, **chose** different colleges.*

Here's a way to say it that puts the doer (the subject, *twins*) closer to what's being done (the verb, *chose*): *The **twins chose** different colleges, after going to the same schools and camps all their lives despite the advice of their parents and teachers.*

If you need a compass to navigate a sentence, take another whack at the writing.

9. Watch out for pronounitis.

A sentence with too many pronouns (*he, him, she, her, it, they, them,* and other words that substitute for nouns) can give your reader hives: *Fleur thinks that Judy told **her** boyfriend about **their** stupid little adventure and that **she** will come to regret **it**.*

Whose boyfriend? Whose stupid little adventure? Who'll regret what?

When you write things like this, of course, you know the cast of characters. It won't be so clear to somebody else. Don't make the reader guess.

10. Make sure there's a time and place for everything.

While the merger specialist was vacationing in Aspen she said she secretly put the squeeze on Mr. Buyout by threatening to go public with candid photos of him in one of those foil helmets, getting his hair streaked at Frederic Fekkai.

Did the merger specialist tell this story when she was vacationing in Aspen, or is that where she put the squeeze on Mr. Buyout? Were the photos taken earlier? And where is Frederic Fekkai? This calls for two sentences:

While vacationing in Aspen, the merger specialist faxed us her secret. She had put the squeeze on Mr. Buyout in New York the week before by threatening to go public with candid photos of him in one of those foil helmets, getting his hair streaked at Frederic Fekkai.

Where are we? What's going on? What time is it? These are questions the reader shouldn't have to ask.

11. Imagine what you're writing.

Picture in your mind any images you've created.

Are they unintentionally funny, like this one? *The bereaved family covered the mirrors as a reflection of its grief.* If you don't see what's wrong, reflect on it for a moment.

Are there too many of them, as in this sentence? *The remaining bone of contention is a thorn in his side and an albatross around his neck.* Give the poor guy a break. One image at a time, please.

12. Put your ideas in order.

Don't make the reader rearrange your messy sentences to figure out what's going on. The parts should follow logically. This doesn't mean they should be rattled off in chronological order, but the sequence of ideas should make sense. Here's how Gracie Allen might have talked about a soufflé recipe, for instance:

It is possible to make this soufflé with four eggs instead of eight. But it will collapse and possibly even catch fire in the oven, leaving you with a flat, burned soufflé. Now, you wouldn't want that, would you? So if you have only four eggs, reduce all the other ingredients in the recipe by half.

Rearrange the ideas:

This soufflé recipe calls for eight eggs. If you want to use fewer, reduce the other ingredients accordingly. If the proportions aren't maintained, the soufflé could flatten or burn.

13. Read with a felonious mind.

Forget the details for a minute. Now step back and take a look at what you've written. Have you said what you wanted to say? After all, leaving the wrong impression is much worse than making a couple of grammatical boo-boos. Get some perspective.

Assuming you've made your point, ask yourself whether you could make it more smoothly. Somebody once said that in good writing, the sentences hold hands. See if you can give yours a helping hand. It may be that by adding or subtracting a word here or there, you could be even clearer. Or you could switch two sentences around, or begin one of them differently.

There's no easy way to raise your writing from competence to artistry. It helps, though, to read with a felonious mind. If you see a letter or memo or report that you admire, read it again. Why do you like it, and what makes it so effective? When you find a technique that works, steal it. Someday, others may be stealing from you.

Glossary

ADJECTIVE. A word describing or characterizing a noun. It can come before the noun (*pink sweater*) or after (*The sweater is pink*). Because an adjective adds something to a noun, it's called a modifier; we say it "modifies" the noun.

ADVERB. A word that describes or characterizes a verb (*He grunted lugubriously*). It can also characterize an adjective (*He is very lugubrious*) or another adverb (*He grunted very lugubriously*). An adverb is called a modifier, because it "modifies" the verb.

APOSTROPHE. A mark of punctuation that's used to make nouns possessive (*Albert's coat*), to form some plurals (*the 1950's*), and to show where letters have been omitted, as in contractions (*wouldn't*).

ARTICLE. The three articles (*a, an, the*) are actually tiny adjectives that tell us whether a noun refers to a particular thing (*the* chair, *the* ottoman) or just one of those things (*a* chair, *an* ottoman). *The* is called the definite article; *a* and *an* are indefinite articles.

BRACKETS. Marks of punctuation used in quoted material or excerpts to enclose something that's not part of the original, like an explanatory aside. *"My weight [154 pounds] is a well-kept secret," said Leona.*

CLAUSE. A group of words with its own subject and verb. A simple sentence might consist of only one clause: *Ernest left for Paris.* More complex sentences have several clauses, as in this example: *I learned | that Ernest left for Paris | when Scott told me.* Independent clauses make sense alone (*I put on a sock . . .*), but dependent, or subordinate, clauses don't (*. . . that had no mate*).

CLICHÉ. A figure of speech that's lost its sparkle. When you find yourself using one, nip it in the bud—or maybe I should put that another way.

COLLECTIVE NOUN. A noun that stands for a group of people or things, like *total* or *number.* It can be considered singular (*The **number** is staggering*) or plural (*A number of them have gone their separate ways*).

COLON. A punctuation mark that can be used to introduce a statement, a series of things, a quotation, or instructions. It's an abrupt stop within a sentence, almost like a period, telling you to brake before going on.

COMMA. A punctuation mark that indicates a pause. If it

were a traffic signal, it would be a yellow light. It can be used to separate clauses in a sentence, or items in a series.

CONDITIONAL CLAUSE. A clause that starts with *if, as if, as though,* or some other expression of supposition. The verb in a conditional clause has an attitude: that is, it takes on different forms, or "moods," depending on the speaker's attitude or intention toward what's being said. When the clause states a condition that's contrary to fact, the verb is in the subjunctive mood (*If I **were** you . . .*). When the clause states a condition that may be true, the verb is in the indicative mood (*If I **was** late . . .*). For more on the conditional, see VERB.

CONJUNCTION. A connecting word. The telltale part of this term is "junction," because that's where a conjunction is found—at the junction where words or phrases or clauses or sentences are joined. The most familiar conjunctions are *and, but,* and *or.* And it's fine to start a sentence with one. But not too often. Or you'll overdo it.

CONSONANT. Generally, a letter with a "hard" sound: *b, c, d, f, g, h, j, k, l, m, n, p, q, r, s, t, v, w, x, y, z.* Sometimes the consonants *w* and *y* act like vowels, which are letters with a "soft," openmouthed sound. And occasionally consonants (such as *g, h,* and others) are seen but not heard.

CONTRACTION. Two words combined into one, with an apostrophe showing where letters are omitted. There are three kinds of contractions: a verb plus *not* (*do + not = don't*); a pronoun plus a verb (*they + are = they're*); and a noun plus a verb (*Bob* + *is* = *Bob's*). Don't confuse the last example with the possessive (*Bob's dog*).

DANGLER. A word or phrase in the wrong place that ends up describing the wrong thing: ***After napping,** the card table was set up.* Who was napping? Unless it's the table, change the sentence: *After napping, Oscar set up the card table.*

DASH. A punctuation mark that interrupts a sentence to insert another thought. One can act like a colon: *It was every mother's nightmare—ringworm.* Or a pair of dashes can be used like parentheses: *The remedy was easy enough—a simple oral medication—but what would she tell the neighbors?*

DICTIONARY. A book that lists words in alphabetical order and gives their meanings, pronunciations, and origins—including words that aren't legit, like *alright*. The fact that a word can be found in the dictionary doesn't mean it's all right. Read the fine print.

DOUBLE NEGATIVE. A double negative is what you get when you combine a negative, or "not," verb with a negative pronoun (like *nothing* or *nobody*), a negative adverb (like *hardly* or *never*), or a negative conjunction (like *neither* or *nor*). Some flagrant examples of double negatives: *I have not seen nobody. It wasn't hardly worth it. He is not there, neither.* Some examples of allowable negative upon negative: *It's not inconceivable. She's not unappealing.*

ELLIPSIS POINTS. Punctuation that indicates an omission, or ellipsis, in a quotation. The three dots can show the omission of a word—in this case a naughty one: *"Get off my* *lawn, and take your . . . dog with you!" he shouted.* Or they can show where a sentence trails off: *"Now let me think. . . ."* Notice that when the ellipsis points come at the end of the sentence, a period precedes them, so you end up with four dots instead of three. (If you want to emphasize the incompleteness of the trailing off, you may end with a space, then just three dots: "But . . .")

EXCLAMATION POINT. A punctuation mark that comes after something that's exclaimed: *"I passed!" said Pippa.* Go easy on the exclamation point and save it for the really startling stuff.

FIGURATIVE. Language is figurative when it uses words in imaginative or out-of-the-ordinary ways. In the process, the truth is often stretched to make a point. If you were being literal, you might say: *Jack's dog is very large.* But to be more vivid, you could say: *Jack's dog is the size of a Shetland pony.*

FIGURE OF SPEECH. An imaginative (or "figurative") expression: *She knows how to push his buttons.* (See FIGURATIVE.) When a figure of speech gets stale, it becomes a cliché.

GERUND. A word that's made of a verb plus *ing* (*bowling,* for example) and that acts as a noun: ***Bowling** is his first love.* The same *ing* word is a participle if it acts as an adjective (*He's a **bowling** fool*) or part of a verb (*He was **bowling***).

GRAMMAR. A system of rules for arranging words into sentences. We adopt rules when we need them and discard them when we don't, so the rules are always changing.

HYPHEN. A mark of punctuation that looks like a stubby dash. It is used to join words together to make new ones (*self-conscious*), and to link syllables when a word, like *hu-mongous* here, breaks off at the end of a line and continues on the next.

IMPERATIVE. A verb is imperative when the speaker is expressing a command or request: *Lose twenty pounds, Jack.* (See MOOD.)

INDICATIVE. A verb is indicative when the speaker is expressing a straightforward statement or question: *Jack lost twenty pounds.* (See MOOD.)

INFINITIVE. A verb in its simplest form (*sneeze,* for example). While the preposition *to* is usually a signal that the infinitive is being used (*to sneeze*), it's not part of the infinitive itself. Putting an adverb in the middle (*to loudly sneeze*) is fine—you're not really "splitting" anything.

INTERJECTION. A word (or words) expressing a sudden rush of feeling: *My word! Help! Wow! Oh, damn!*

INTERROGATIVE. An expression is interrogative if it asks a question.

INTRANSITIVE. See VERB.

JARGON. Language used by windbags and full of largely meaningless, pseudotechnical terms that are supposed to lend the speaker an aura of expertise. The advantage of jargon is that you can use it to discuss things you know little about, and without saying anything. *Jargon* comes from an old word for "chattering" or "twittering."

LITERAL. True or "to the letter"—the opposite of figurative. Don't use the adverb *literally* to modify a figure of speech, as in: *The boss literally had kittens.*

METAPHOR. The most common figure of speech. A metaphor takes the language normally used for one thing and applies it to something else: *His stomach began to growl. The moon was a silver coin upon the water.*

MOOD. Verbs have attitude. They take on different forms, called *moods,* or sometimes *modes,* that reflect the speaker's attitude toward what's being said. There are three moods in English. If what's being said is an ordinary statement or question about facts, the verb is in the indicative mood. (*He is on my foot.*) If what's being said is contrary to fact or expresses a wish, the verb is in the subjunctive mood. (*I wish he were not on my foot. If he were not on my foot, I could go.*) If what's being said is a command or a request, the verb is in the imperative mood. (*Get off my foot!*)

NOUN. A word that stands for a person, place, thing, or idea. A common noun starts with a small letter (*city* or *girl* or *religion,* for example); a proper noun starts with a capital letter (*Memphis* or *Molly* or *Methodist*).

OBJECT. A noun or pronoun that's acted on by a verb. It can be something you give, for instance, or somebody you give it to. An indirect object is the person or thing on the receiving end of the action, and a direct object is who or what ends up there: *Harry gave me* [indirect object] *the flu* [direct object]. Think of it like a game of catch—you throw a direct object to an indirect object.

Additionally, a noun or pronoun at the receiving end of a preposition (*to* and *from* in these examples) is an object: *Harry gave the flu to me. He is from Chicago.*

PARENTHESES. Marks of punctuation used to enclose an aside—either whole sentences or words within a sentence.

PARTS OF SPEECH. The eight kinds of words: noun, pronoun, adjective, verb, adverb, preposition, conjunction, interjection. This sentence uses all of them: *But* [conjunction] *gosh* [interjection], *you* [pronoun] *are* [verb] *really* [adverb] *in* [preposition] *terrible* [adjective] *trouble* [noun]*!*

PERIOD. A punctuation mark that shows where a declarative sentence, one that states something, ends. The period is also used in abbreviations (U.S. for "United States," M.D. for "medical doctor").

PHRASE. A group of related words that doesn't have a subject and verb, like *glorious sunset* or *in the meantime* or *to spill the beans* or *gently swinging in the breeze.* A group of words with both a subject and its verb is a clause.

PLURAL. More than one; just one is singular. Plural nouns generally have endings different from singular ones (*berries* versus *berry,* for example).

POSSESSIVE. Showing ownership. With most nouns, you get the possessive form (or "case") by adding *'s* (*Alice's cousin*) or the preposition *of* (*a cousin of Alice*). A "double possessive" uses both methods (*a cousin of Alice's*).

PREPOSITION. A word that "positions" or situates words in relation to one another. The roots of the term *preposition* mean "put before," which is appropriate, because a preposition usually comes before a noun or pronoun: *My cousin is from Philly.* (Contrary to what you might have heard, however, it can indeed go at the end of a sentence.) The prepositions we use most are *about, above, across, after, against, ahead of, along, among, around, as, at, away from, before, behind, below, beneath, beside, between, but* (in the sense of "except"), *by, down, except, for, from, in, in back of, in front of, inside, into, like, of, off, on, onto, out, out of, outside, over, past, since, through, throughout, to, toward, under, until, up, upon, with, within, without.* Some of these words can serve as other parts of speech as well (adverbs, conjunctions).

PRONOUN. A word that can be used in place of a noun. Pronouns fall into these categories:

- A **personal pronoun** can be a subject (*I, you, he, she, it, we, they*); an object (*me, you, him, her, it, us, them*); or a possessive (*my, mine, your, yours, his, her, hers, its, our, ours, their, theirs*). Some of these (*my, your, his, her, its, our, their*) are also called possessive adjectives, since they describe (or modify) nouns.

- A **reflexive pronoun** calls attention to itself (it ends with *self* or *selves*): *myself, yourself, himself, herself, itself, ourselves, yourselves, themselves.* Reflexive pronouns are used to emphasize (*She **herself** is Hungarian*) or to refer back to the subject (*He blames **himself***).

- A **demonstrative pronoun** points out something: *this, that, these, those.* It can be used by itself (*Hold **this***) or with a noun, as an adjective (*Who is **this** guy?*).

- An **indefinite pronoun** refers to a vague or unknown person or thing: *all, another, any, anybody, anyone, any-*

thing, both, each, either, every, everybody, everyone, every-thing, few, many, much, neither, no one, nobody, none, one, other, several, some, somebody, someone, something, such (**All** *is lost*). Some of these, too, can serve as adjectives.

• An **interrogative pronoun** is used to ask a question: *what, which, who, whom, whose* (**Who**'s *on first?*).

• A **relative pronoun** introduces a dependent (or subordinate) clause: *that, what, whatever, which, whichever, who, whoever, whom, whomever, whose* (*He's the guy* **who** *stole my heart*).

PUNCTUATION. The signs and signals in writing that direct the traffic of language. They call for stops, starts, slowdowns, and detours. The marks of punctuation include the period, the comma, the colon, the semicolon, the question mark, the exclamation point, the apostrophe, the dash, the hyphen, parentheses, ellipsis points, and quotation marks.

QUESTION MARK. A punctuation mark that comes at the end of a question.

QUOTATION MARKS. Punctuation marks that surround spoken or quoted words.

SEMICOLON. A punctuation mark for a stop that's less final than a period. It's like a flashing red light—it lets you drive on after a brief pause. You'll often find it between clauses in a sentence and between items in a series.

SENTENCE. A word or group of words that expresses a complete thought; in writing, it begins with a capital letter and ends with a concluding mark (period, question mark, or exclamation point). Most sentences have a subject and a verb, but not all. An imperative sentence, which demands an action, may have only a verb (*Run!*). An interrogative sentence, which asks a question, may also have only one word (*How?*). An exclamatory sentence, which expresses emotion, may have only a word or phrase (*Good heavens!*). The declarative sentence, the most common kind, conveys information and is likely to have a subject, a verb, and an object—usually in that order: *He ate my fries.*

SIBILANT. A consonant sound that hisses, like *s, z, sh, zh, ch,* and *j.* Nouns that end in sibilants sometimes have special ways of forming plurals and possessives.

SINGULAR. Only one; more than one is plural. A noun or a verb is singular if it applies to a single person, place, or thing.

STUFFED SHIRT. A person likely to use jargon; similar to a windbag. (See JARGON.)

SUBJECT. That which initiates an action; in other words, who or what is doing whatever's being done. Subjects can be nouns (like *Harry*), pronouns (like *I*), or phrases (like *Harry and I*). *Good old **Harry and I** have fallen arches.* A subject with all its accessories (*Good old Harry and I*) is the complete subject. One stripped to its bare essentials (*Harry and I*) is the simple or basic subject.

SUBJUNCTIVE. A verb is in the subjunctive (see MOOD) when the intention is to express:

1. A wish (*I wish Jack **were** here*).

2. A conditional (*if*) statement that's untrue (*If Jack were here . . .*).

3. A suggestion or demand (*We insist that Jack be here*).

Syllable. Part of a word that is pronounced as a single unit. The word *syllable* has three syllables: SIL-la-bul. *Word* is a one-syllable word.

Tense. What a verb uses to tell time. The basic tenses— present, past, future—and the variations on them tell us when an action takes place, took place, will take place, and so on. We're always telling time with verbs, since whenever we use one, there's a "when" built in. See VERB for examples of some common verb forms at work.

Transitive. See VERB.

Verb. An action word. In a sentence, it tells you what's going on: *She sells seashells*. Verbs are called transitive when they need an object to make sense (*Henry raises dahlias*) and intransitive when they make sense without one (*Flowers die*). Also see MOOD and TENSE.

Here's what some common verb forms look like, for the first person singular (*I*) and the verb *eat*.

	PRESENT	PAST	FUTURE	CONDITIONAL
SIMPLE	I eat	I ate	I will eat	I would eat
PROGRESSIVE	I am eating	I was eating	I will be eating	I would be eating
PERFECT	I have eaten	I had eaten	I will have eaten	I would have eaten

Vowel. A letter with a "soft," openmouthed sound: *a, e, i, o, u*. The other letters are consonants; two of them, *w* and *y*, sometimes act like vowels.

Bibliography

Here are some books that have helped me. You may find them helpful, too. (A dictionary isn't optional, though. It's required.)

The Careful Writer: A Modern Guide to English Usage. Theodore M. Bernstein. New York: Atheneum, 1977.

A Dictionary of Contemporary American Usage. Bergen Evans and Cornelia Evans. New York: Random House, 1957.

A Dictionary of Modern English Usage. H. W. Fowler. 2nd ed., revised by Ernest Gowers. New York: Oxford University Press, 1965.

The Elements of Style. William Strunk, Jr., and E. B. White. 3rd ed. New York: Macmillan, 1979.

Essentials of English Grammar. Otto Jespersen. Tuscaloosa: University of Alabama Press, 1964.

Harper's English Grammar. John B. Opdycke. Revised ed. New York: Warner, 1983.

The Language Instinct. Steven Pinker. New York: Morrow, 1994.

Modern American Usage: A Guide. Wilson Follett. Edited and completed by Jacques Barzun et al. New York: Hill & Wang, 1966.

The New York Public Library Writer's Guide to Style and Usage. Edited by Andrea J. Sutcliffe. New York: Harper-Collins, 1994.

Plain Words: Their ABC. Ernest Gowers. New York: Knopf, 1954.

Simple & Direct: A Rhetoric for Writers. Jacques Barzun. Revised ed. Chicago: University of Chicago Press, 1994.

Style: Toward Clarity and Grace. Joseph M. Williams. Chicago: University of Chicago Press, 1990.

Words into Type. Marjorie E. Skillin, Robert M. Gay, et al. 3rd ed. Englewood Cliffs, NJ: Prentice-Hall, 1974.

DICTIONARIES

The American Heritage Dictionary of the English Language. 3rd ed. Boston: Houghton Mifflin, 1996.

Merriam-Webster's Collegiate Dictionary. 10th ed. Springfield, MA: Merriam-Webster, 1996.

Random House Webster's College Dictionary. New York: Random House, 1996.

Webster's New World College Dictionary. 3rd ed. New York: Macmillan, 1996.

Index